7 LONDON in DAYS

LUCY MCMURDO

NEW HOLLAND

CONTENTS

To my family: Mac, Ben & Jo for their tolerance,
love and invaluable support.

INTRODUCTION

London in seven days. What an impossible task! How can anyone manage to fit in everything that London has to offer in this time? Both as a bustling, prosperous 21st century world city, and with over 2,000 years of history in its streets and buildings, London is a really vibrant place with so much appeal regardless of your age or background.

It is a truly multi-cultural city with every kind of activity and cuisine available. So many different nationalities live here that the city is a complete melting pot and it is not unusual to find Chinese Opera, see a Brazilian dance troupe or visit a Russian winter festival in and around its main streets. Londoners and visitors alike enjoy and take pleasure in the city's diversity, its festivals and celebrations.

As you would expect from a city of its size, London is constantly changing, moving forward with new areas emerging and making their mark. Often places that had been thought to be down-and-out, seedy, neglected or industrial are now considered the most chic, cool and trendy places to see and be seen in.

East London in particular, has been going through a wonderful makeover. The decision to build the London 2012 Olympic Stadium and Village in Stratford, north-east London gave a huge impetus to this area. With vastly improved transport links you can now reach King's Cross from Stratford in seven minutes or take the tube or London Overground into central London. The district has been revitalized, and has excellent sport and recreational facilities in the nearby Queen Elizabeth Olympic Park, Theater Royal Stratford East and the Westfield Shopping Centre.

The villages immediately east of the City of London have also grown immensely in popularity: Hoxton, Shoreditch, Brick Lane and Spitalfields are no longer taboo areas and they attract huge crowds day and night, to their restaurants, galleries, markets, entertainment venues, themed bars and shops.

Naturally, such a developing city requires the very best infrastructure possible and so London's transport is continually under review. The work on Crossrail linking east and west London is racing ahead whilst many of the tube and Overground lines are being upgraded. As much of this work takes place on weekends be sure to check on the Transport for London (TfL) website (*www.tfl.gov.uk*) for details of possible line closures. It is also the site to obtain excellent up-to-the-minute information about all of London's public transport.

Information about useful websites and transport into London (from airports and ports) and around the city is given at the end of the book. Here you will also find details about the Oyster Card and other methods of payment used on London's Underground, buses, trams, DLR, Overground, riverboats and National Railway.

London in Seven Days is a guidebook packed with information and recommendations about London's major sites and destinations plus some less well-known or visited secret 'treasures' often missed in an initial visit. It is the ideal guidebook if you are visiting the capital for the first time or on a return trip. Unlike many other books on the market it does not set out to provide lists of accommodation or restaurants but is intended wholly as a guide to what is on and where to go in London.

You will discover a range of areas like: Bankside – home to Shakespeare's Globe Theater and Tate Modern; tourist hotspots Covent Garden, Soho and Chinatown; Royal parks and palaces; the famous 'Square Mile'; London's four UNESCO World Heritage Sites – the Tower of London, Maritime Greenwich, the Palace of Westminster and the Royal Botanic Gardens at Kew.

In addition, a varied selection of London's museums and galleries are included in the book describing the world-famous collections of the British Museum, the Tate art galleries and the South Kensington museums. Many of these are free, open daily and some offer late-night opening too. Children love the Natural History Museum's dinosaur and Creepy Crawlies galleries, the interactive displays in the Science Museum, and get great delight out of trying their hand at being London tube train drivers at the London Transport Museum.

London in Seven Days describes what is on offer in London today. Whether you are visiting for culture, sport, history, shopping or to see the iconic sites, it gives you heaps of ideas of how to spend your time in the city. You will find information about major attractions and 'behind the scenes' tours at London theaters and concert halls, a visit to the Inns of Court, ice-skating at Somerset House and the many festivals held along the South Bank. In addition there are sections devoted to London's nightlife: its theaters, clubs, concerts, themed bars, rooftop dining, restaurants and cocktail bar venues.

If the pace of city life gets too much, remember that there are many places where you can take time out – in parks, gardens, churchyards, piazzas and alongside the river and canals. It is sometimes said that London is an expensive city but take advantage of the multitude of cafes and restaurants away from the main tourist spots, use local supermarkets and coffee shops and you will not exceed your budget! Remember too that not only are many attractions free but where a charge is made it usually costs less if you book beforehand on the internet. If you are extremely well organized you will also find great bargains on many restaurant booking sites especially for lunch time set menus.

HOW TO USE THE BOOK

The book is divided into **seven themed days**, which can be followed in any order, dependent upon individual tastes. Each day is divided into **two sections**, with each containing at least three activities or places to visit. **Section One** suggests activities for the first time visitor, whilst **Section Two** is aimed at repeat travelers. However, there is nothing stopping you from mixing and matching!

In addition to the **seven themed days** there are information panels inserted in the text containing details of London's festivals, theaters, bars, restaurants and nightlife, parks and villages. There is also a panel with suggestions for short day trips away from London.

I have omitted opening hours and attraction fees as these change from time to time and it is best to check online for current information. A section containing useful web addresses relating to each chapter can be found at the end of the book. Here, you will also find a glossary with explanations of historical periods and architectural terms referred to in the text.

Last word

As a Londoner, Blue Badge London Tourist Guide and Guide Trainer I am totally in love with London, its landmarks, culture and atmosphere. Each and every day spent in the capital is exciting and there are always new places to visit and events to experience. I am aware that this book is only the tip of the iceberg in terms of what there is to see and do in London. However, it is a start, and I hope that you enjoy whatever you choose to do. A good tip worth remembering: you don't have to cover everything, and it may be a lot more agreeable to do less but get to know the ways of the city more, to experience how London works and how the locals live. In any case, what you don't fit in to your itinerary this time can be top of your list on a subsequent visit!

So, all that is left for me to say is 'have fun' on your visit and come back soon!

DAY 1

Around Westminster and Whitehall

SECTION ONE

PARLIAMENTARY, ROYAL AND RELIGIOUS WESTMINSTER

PARLIAMENT SQUARE

In reality Parliament Square is a traffic island bounded by Westminster Abbey, the Supreme Court, government buildings and the Palace of Westminster. It has been spruced up considerably in recent years after a period of general neglect, and is now the place to visit memorial statues of global leaders such as Sir Winston Churchill, Mahatma Gandhi, Nelson Mandela, Abraham Lincoln plus a host of British Prime Ministers of the 19th century.

The square, although both chaotic and noisy, is a wonderful spot to view Big Ben (Elizabeth Tower) and for taking photos of London's most iconic landmarks – that is, if you are able to find a gap in the traffic and are not obstructed by one of the many red buses or black taxi cabs!

Exit Parliament Square on its north-east side passing by the Royal Institution of Chartered Surveyors (just behind Lincoln's monument), and turn left into Great George Street. Cross over the roadway and stand on the perimeter of St James's Park.

St James's Park and Changing the Guard

You are now standing on Birdcage Walk, so named because it was home to a Royal aviary and menagerie during the 1600s in the reign of King James I. When St James's Park was landscaped in the latter years of the century the aviary was enlarged and today the name remains appropriate as the nearby lake is stocked with birds, ducks and pelicans (a gift from the Russian Ambassador in 1664). You can see a delightful cottage which is home to the official 'Keeper of the Birds' and if you choose to visit between 2.30pm and 3pm you'll get to see the birds being fed fresh fish. Wonderfully entertaining, the pelicans are often found sitting on the many benches beside the lake sharing the space with visitors and lunch-time office workers.

Walk along Birdcage Walk until you reach a path on your right, then follow this into the park and on to the bridge that crosses the lake. It may be a little crowded on the bridge but if possible stop in the middle and look over to your right. From here you have a great view of Horse Guards Parade, the Italianate style tower of the Foreign and Commonwealth Office and catch a glimpse of the London Eye (officially named the Coca-Cola London Eye) as well as Big Ben. Turn your head in the other direction and you will be looking directly at the monarch's London home, Buckingham Palace. It is here that the Changing the Guard ceremony takes place on the palace forecourt (daily April–August, and every other day for the remainder of the year). If the Royal Standard (comprised of four quarterings, with three lions passant, a lion rampant and a harp) is flying above the palace then the Queen is in residence; when the Union Flag (red, blue and white) is raised she is not at home.

Continue across the bridge and follow the path up to the large iron gates. The road directly in front of you is The Mall, the official processional route which leads from Trafalgar Square to Buckingham Palace. Almost immediately opposite you (slightly to the left) is St James's Palace and it is from here at 11.15am that the Old Guard stationed at the palace will march along the Mall on to the forecourt of

Buckingham Palace, generally accompanied by a band. This is pageantry at its best! Soldiers bedecked in their summer or winter uniforms, sporting bearskins, tunics and symbols denoting their troop, and marching in time to the music – a real spectacle.

Follow the guards as they move along the Mall and stop as close as you can get to Buckingham Palace to see the ceremony. The old guard will shortly be joined on the Palace forecourt by the new contingent of guards from the Wellington Barracks (alongside the park), who will relieve the old sentries of their duties.

Whilst the soldiers are lined up on the forecourt you'll see the equally splendid display of the Household Cavalry riding along The Mall from the guard change ceremony at Horse Guards en route to their Hyde Park barracks. At the end of the Buckingham Palace Guard Change ceremony some of the soldiers will

remain at the palace whilst others march back to St James's Palace to take up duty there. The whole ceremony is complete by about midday and the area becomes peaceful again!

Now, turn back into St James's Park and walk alongside the lake. When you reach the bridge turn right and follow the pathway out on to Birdcage Walk. Cross the road at the lights, and continue straight ahead through the iron gates until you see St James's Park Underground Station in front of you. Above the station is a striking art-deco building which, until recently, was the Headquarters of London Transport. Designed by Charles Holden (responsible for many London Underground stations, signage, artwork and décor) it was considered very modern when it was built in the late 1920s and was the tallest office in London at that time! As you pass the building look up to see its impressive statue reliefs, the work of avant-garde sculptors of the day such as Jacob Epstein, Eric Gill and Henry Moore.

Turn left into Tothill Street, which leads you to Westminster Abbey, your next stop. Around this area you will find a number of pubs, coffee shops, restaurants and cafes all suitable for a lunch-time break.

WESTMINSTER ABBEY

Also called the Collegiate Church of St Peter at Westminster, the Abbey was originally part of a monastery built on a marshy area of Thorney Island beside the Thames. The church was commissioned by Edward the Confessor, ruler of England from 1042–1066. A very pious man he wanted to build a church befitting his god. In order to oversee the building works he had a palace built for himself close by which in later years came to be used as the seat of Parliament, the Administration and the law courts.

The main body of Westminster Abbey is Gothic in style and dates from the 13th century. In contrast the West Front with its twin towers and massive doorway was added five hundred years later and built in the Baroque style. The West Front is recognized the world over because it is where events at the Abbey are televised; most recently in 2011, the wedding of Prince William to Catherine Middleton. The Queen's marriage to Prince Philip in 1947 took place here and it is where she was crowned as monarch in 1953. Since its birth, Westminster Abbey has been the church of coronations, where all bar two English monarchs (Edward V and Edward VIII) have been crowned and is home to the 800-year-old Coronation Chair. Fourteen queens and thirteen kings are buried within its confines, but having run out of space, royal burials since the 19th century have taken place in St George's Chapel and at Frogmore House in Windsor instead.

The Abbey is very much a living church, holding 29 services a week. Additional services of thanksgiving for the lives of notable figures such as Lord Richard Attenborough, Lady Soames (Churchill's daughter) and Sir David Frost have also taken place here in recent years.

The Abbey's stunning interior is a delight of Gothic architecture with its high lofty ceilings, narrow columns and pointed arched windows, and the entire building is full of statues, memorials, tombs and plaques. Many people from the world of politics, the arts, sciences and literature are remembered within its precincts and there are areas devoted to musicians, scientists, engineers, statesmen, as well as poets, authors, composers and actors. Geoffrey Chaucer, the 14th century author of *The Canterbury Tales* not only spent time in the king's service holding the post of 'Clerk of the Works at the Palace of Westminster' but also lived close to the Abbey which qualified him for an Abbey burial. His remains were moved to the present site in 1556, and when Edmund Spenser, the Elizabethan poet died in 1599 and was buried near to Chaucer, the development of 'Poets' Corner' within the Abbey was established.

Today, Poets' Corner is full of memorials and burials ranging from poets of World War I to American authors such as Longfellow and T. S. Eliot. Shakespeare, the Romantic poets, Kipling, Handel, Dickens, Sir Laurence Olivier as well as Jane Austen, Mrs Gaskell and the Bronte sisters are all represented here.

Some major highlights of the Abbey are the tomb of the Unknown Warrior, the shrine of Edward the Confessor, the magnificent Cosmati pavement in front of the altar, and the Lady Chapel, with its exquisite fan-vaulted ceiling along with Torrigiano's tomb of King Henry VII and his queen. Nearby are the tombs of Queen Elizabeth I and her half-sister Mary Tudor, strangely together in death, despite being quite at odds during their lifetimes.

There is so much to see that it is easy to spend several hours within the church alone, but if possible, do find the time to explore the cloisters too. This was the area where the monks worked, studied and lived when the Abbey was first built in the late 11th century. From here you can see the sturdy flying buttresses which give support to the structure and are required because of the height of the building and the span of the roof. Off the cloisters you can enter the elegant octagonal Chapter House where the monks would have gathered each morning to read one of the 73 chapters of the Rule of St Benedict – which is how the name 'Chapter House' was coined. Over the centuries this space has been used both as a meeting place for the King's Great Council of the House of Commons, and as a national archive centre, home to the Domesday Book and Magna Carta (now to be found at the British Library alongside St Pancras Railway Station).

Next, pop into the Abbey Museum in the crypt next door to the Chapter House. It contains a most interesting collection of medieval wooden effigies as well as wax figures of royal and noble persons of the late 17th century, including Charles II, William III and Mary II and Queen Anne. It also displays the death masks of Edward III and Henry VII, the Westminster Retable (the oldest surviving 13th century altarpiece c.1270) and a replica set of Crown Jewels used at the rehearsal for George IV's coronation.

A lovely backwater is the Monk's garden at the far end of the cloisters. Open on Tuesday, Wednesday and Thursday it is where the monks once grew herbs for medicinal purposes and is a wonderful quiet oasis. Situated right beside the celebrated Westminster School you may even catch sight of some of the pupils. One of Britain's top schools it has a large number of famous alumni: Sir Christopher Wren, Andrew Lloyd-Webber, Henry Purcell, Sir John Gielgud,

Nigella Lawson, Helena Bonham-Carter and Martha Lane-Cox.

Before exiting the cloisters and the Abbey precincts there is a small shop and café. Outside by the Abbey's west front is a much larger shop with a great range of gifts and books.

THE PALACE OF WESTMINSTER AND THE HOUSES OF PARLIAMENT

The Palace of Westminster was the main residence of English monarchs from the mid-11th century for about 450 years and where Medieval kings summoned their courts. It has been the seat of parliament since the mid-13th century when Simon de Montfort summoned shire representatives to Westminster Hall, and by the end of the 1300s the judiciary, administration and parliament were all located here.

Despite its somewhat deceptive appearance the current palace is less than 200 years old, dating from the 1840s. Totally reconstructed in a neo-Gothic style after a devastating fire in 1834 its architecture is remarkably similar to the Lady Chapel of Westminster Abbey opposite, despite there being a three hundred year gap in time between their construction!

A competition to design the new palace was held and the contract was awarded to Victorian architect Charles Barry and draughtsman Augustus Welby Pugin. It was their vision and Barry's design that were so successful in the construction of the new Parliament building which contains approximately 1,100 rooms, 11 courtyards, 100 staircases and over 4.8 kilometres (3 miles) of passages.

The present procedure of the House of Commons and House of Lords sitting in the building began in the 1540s and has continued ever since. Very little remains today of the medieval buildings except for Westminster Hall, the cloisters and Chapter House of St Stephen's and the Undercroft chapel.

Entry to the Palace of Westminster may be by several routes; through tours of Parliament, attending committees and debates, visiting the parliamentary archives, attending parliamentary events, or even a wedding ceremony! A number of different tours are available ranging from Member of Parliament (MP) organised Palace tours, self-guided audio tours and a 90 minute guided tour around the Palace. To make it a really special occasion you can take afternoon tea on the Terrace pavilion and enjoy splendid views of the Thames (though an extra charge is made for this).

During the spring and summer further tours may be offered focusing on the artwork within the House of Lords, or perhaps the contemporary portraiture within Portcullis House. Every Saturday throughout the year and during the Parliamentary recesses at Easter and in the summer, Parliamentary tours conducted by expert London Blue Badge Tourist Guides are also offered in French, German, Italian, Spanish, Russian and Mandarin.

Joining a tour is an excellent way to see the Palace interior and to find out about the workings of the UK Parliament. You will visit the Queen's Robing Room, the Royal Gallery, the Central Lobby, the Lords Chamber and the Commons Chamber where you see the woolsack, the Sovereign's Throne and Speaker's Chair. Discover the reason for the layout of the Commons and visit the lobby areas where MPs cast their vote. The tour concludes via St Stephen's Hall (once home to the Commons) and Westminster Hall.

Westminster Hall is all that remains of the original 11th century palace. Built at the north end of the Palace by William Rufus, (son of William the Conqueror) it has been in use for 900 years. Originally, a venue for feasting and entertainments, it later became the forerunner of the present House of Lords. It was here in 1265, that the first English parliament with elected representatives met, summoned by Simon de Montfort. At this time, it boasted the largest hall in Europe – which helped to make it the Administrative and Judicial centre of the kingdom. It is still renowned for its cavernous size, its ancient walls (1097–99), and its wonderful unsupported oak hammer-beam roof, designed in the reign of Richard II (late 1300s), the work of Henry Yvele.

A number of State trials were heard within the Hall – including that of **Charles I, Thomas More and Guy Fawkes**. Also, in later centuries Westminster Hall was home to the Courts of Law.

Today, the Hall is used for public ceremonies, such as an address by a distinguished Head of State; President de Gaulle (1960), Nelson Mandela (1996) Pope Benedict XVI (2010) have all spoken here.

In recent years, the Hall was the venue for the lying-in-state of **Queen Elizabeth, the Queen Mother** (2002). Other lyings-in-state include: **Winston Churchill** (1965), **George VI** (1952), **Queen Mary** (1953), **George V** (1936), **Edward VII** (1910) and **William Gladstone** (1898).

LONDON AT NIGHT

Like every major capital city London really comes alive at night and it is particularly attractive at dusk when buildings, trees and the riverside are all lit up.

The choice of activities is enormous and there is never a shortage of things to do; every type of spoken theater production imaginable is on offer along with opera, musicals, dance and performance art. Many museums and art galleries open late one night a week and some hold lectures, workshops, and provide music, bars and refreshments too. During the summer months, it has becoming increasingly popular for films or sporting fixtures to be shown on giant screens

in piazzas, at the **Scoop** alongside City Hall (close by Tower Bridge) and at major attractions such as **Somerset House** and **Covent Garden**.

In addition concerts are held nightly at arts centres, in churches and at other major venues such as the **Royal Albert Hall,** the **O2 Centre**, **Wigmore Hall, and King's Place**. All over London there are clubs specializing in different music genres, nightclubs, casinos, pubs, gastro-pubs, coffee shops, restaurants and bars. The list is endless! So are the multitude of areas where you can go. The **West End** with Leicester Square, Piccadilly, Covent Garden and Trafalgar Square is a real honeypot but there are plenty of other areas that people flock to. **Brick Lane** is renowned for its excellent Bengali Indian restaurants, whilst areas like **Hoxton** and **Shoreditch** are real hubs of entertainment, remaining open well into the early hours of the morning.

You'll find casinos in **Mayfair** and **Knightsbridge** as well as fine dining and private clubs. **Soho**, once renowned for its sex shops, prostitutes and sleazy ambiance, is now more an area to visit for lively and interesting street life, its gay scene, numerous eateries, pubs, music and clubs. Not that the seedy aspect has completely disappeared – come here late evening and you will see quite a different side of the district though perhaps tamer than it once was.

Areas like the **Edgware Road** and **Queensway** are full of Arabic and Asian restaurants, **Chinatown** near Soho, is the centre for Cantonese and Mandarin food whilst Vietnamese cuisine is the mainstay of **Kingsland Road**, Shoreditch. You will find numerous Turkish restaurants in nearby Dalston.

Jazz enthusiasts are sure to find **Ronnie Scott's** in Frith Street, Soho, one of London's celebrated institutions. In the West End, **Mahiki** round the corner from Green Park tube, is a really popular party destination and cocktail bar visited by a host of celebrities, royals as well as the general public. Slightly further east, in Smithfield is **Fabric**, boasting

three separate rooms, one of which has a vibrating floor, whilst the **Ministry of Sound** is one of London's major nightclubs south of the river near Elephant and Castle.

THEATERS AND THEATERLAND

'Theaterland' is the term coined to describe the mass of theaters sited within a ten minute walk of one another in the very heart of London. It is centred largely around The Strand, Covent Garden, Shaftesbury Avenue, Charing Cross Road, and St Martin's Lane although is extends throughout most of the West End, and is said to be the greatest concentration of theaters in the world! The great majority of theaters are mainstream, some based in buildings that are marvellous examples of Art Deco, others, boast Regency, Victorian and Edwardian architecture, and some like the Soho Theater are relatively new. On account of their wonderful features and decoration, many of the Victorian and Edwardian theaters have been designated listed buildings ensuring that these iconic buildings will be neither demolished nor replaced.

Not only do many of the theaters occupy magnificent buildings but they also provide the most amazing selection of theatrical entertainments ranging from straight drama to thrillers, musicals, ballet, dance and opera. Everyday, more alternative and fringe theaters appear too, giving even greater choice and allowing audiences to become involved in experimental theater.

The **Arts Centres on the South Bank** (Southbank Centre and the National Theater,) as well as the **Barbican** complex in the City of London are other major theater venues and being purpose-built in the 20th century provide comfortable seating in their auditoriums and greater communal spaces.

London's theater really caters for everyone, regardless of background or age. Its stunning epic musicals are famous the world over for their excellent melodies, scenery, costumes and choreography and some like Les Miserables and the Lion King have been running for many years.

To help you find the right venue the list below is a short guide to the specialisms of some of London's theaters:

Kids:

The Unicorn Theater, (London Bridge) National Theater, (Southbank) Little Angel Theater, and Sadler's Wells Theater, (Islington), Half Moon Theater, (Limehouse)

Dance/Performance Art:

Sadler's Wells (Islington), Southbank Centre, Peacock Theater (Holborn), The Roundhouse (Camden)

Opera:

Royal Opera House (Covent Garden), London Coliseum, English National Opera (St Martin's Lane)

Fringe and Alternative:

Soho Theater (Dean Street), The Almeida (Islington), Hampstead Theater, (Swiss Cottage), The Menier Chocolate Factory and Southwark Theater (Southwark), the Arcola (Dalston), St James's Theater (Westminster), the Tricycle Theater (Kilburn), Theater Royal Stratford East (Stratford), Royal Court Theater (Sloane Square)

Shakespeare:

Shakespeare's Globe Theater and Sam Wanamaker Playhouse (Bankside), the Barbican Theater, National Theater, plus many fringe and West End theater productions

Pub Theater:

King's Head, the Hen & Chicken and Old Red Lion Theaters, (Islington), White Bear Theater (Kennington), Upstairs at the Gatehouse (Highgate), Drayton Arms, (Earl's Court)

SECTION TWO

WALKING TOUR OF WESTMINSTER

1. Big Ben and the Elizabeth Tower

Big Ben is one of the most famous features of the Palace of Westminster, and its name refers to the huge bell within the Clock Tower, re-named the Elizabeth Tower in 2012, to commemorate Queen Elizabeth's Diamond Jubilee.

Big Ben came into operation in 1859, weighs7 tonnes, is 2.7 metres wide and 2.3 metres high (8.8 x 7.5 feet). There are 334 steps up to the top of the belfry, and 59 more to the Ayrton Light at the top of the lantern. Augustus Pugin, who worked with Charles Barry on the Palace of Westminster designed the Tower in the Gothic Revival style before his descent into apparent madness and premature death in 1852.

The original bell (16 tons) was manufactured in the north-east of England and brought to London by ship. Unfortunately it cracked during testing, so was recast at nearby Whitechapel Foundry, which still remains in existence today in the East End. As the bell was too large to raise it up the Tower's shaft upright it was winched on its side up to the top, taking 30 hours to reach its destination!

The clock mechanism weighs 5 tonnes, and in Victorian times it required two men to wind it up, three times a week. Even though the clock has been motorised for about 100 years the winding up procedure is still partially carried out manually three times a week on Monday, Wednesday and Friday.

The clock dials are 7 m (23 ft) across and when lit up can be seen from as far as 16 km (10 mi) away! They are externally cleaned every 5 years when cleaners abseil down from the Belfry above. When the House is sitting at night a light is evident on the top of the Belfry.

Big Ben is undoubtedly one of London's most iconic landmarks and film locations. It has been used in numerous adverts, posters, guide leaflets and films. It is most famous perhaps for *The 39 Steps*, but also seen in *V for Vendetta*, *Thunderball* and *Dr Who*.

The chimes are world famous, having been used in both the World Service Radio and on UK BBC radio to herald

the time. Before the annual Remembrance Day service in November, and again at New Year the bells chime out. Most recently, a series of 30 chimes were heard in 3 minutes at the start of the 2012 London Olympics.

2. Whitehall, the Palace and the Cenotaph

Whitehall is generally regarded as the heart of British government, and today is home to many of the government departments such as the Treasury, Foreign Office, Admiralty, Energy and Climate Change, Ministry of Defence, Ministry of Health as well as the Scotland Office and the Wales Office. It takes its name from **Whitehall Palace**, the 16th century royal residence, situated here between the 1530s and the end of the 17th century. A 'White Hall', then being the term used to describe any grand hall designed for festivities.

In 1530, King Henry VIII seized York House from Cardinal Wolsey, his most powerful minister and the Archbishop of York, who had lost the King's favour. Renaming it the Palace of Whitehall, King Henry VIII made it into his chief London palace and used it as his principal residence.

Never one to be outshone King Henry VIII added sumptuous state apartments, tennis courts, a cock-pit, bowling alley, wine cellars and tilt yard. The palace became one of the largest in Europe, almost like a mini-city, and extended 23 acres.

Henry's daughters also enjoyed the Palace (Mary more than Elizabeth, who preferred Greenwich), and in the 17th century the Stuart kings kept it as the seat of government, too. Charles I was actually executed at the Palace, (on a scaffold outside the Banqueting House), while Charles II died of natural causes there.

By 1650 the Palace with its 1,500 rooms was the largest complex of secular buildings in England, larger than both the Vatican and Versailles! Made up of buildings of different ages and architectural styles the palace was very higgledy-piggledy and appeared more of a town than a palace.

Only when fire gutted Whitehall Palace in 1698 did it cease to be used as a Royal residence. At this time the real source of power was with Parliament at Westminster yet to this day Whitehall remains as the home of government offices and administration.

In the middle of the street is the **Cenotaph Memorial** where a ceremony is held each year to remember the war dead on the Sunday closest to 11th November, at 11am. This memorial, the work of Edwin Lutyens, stands opposite the Department of Health. Its name is derived from the Greek 'kenos' (empty) and 'taphos' (tomb). Her Majesty (HM) the Queen, members of the Royal Family, politicians, representatives of the armed forces and war veterans all attend the ceremony and the monarch places a wreath of red poppies at the foot of the cenotaph.

3. Downing Street

This is certainly one of the most exclusive streets in Britain. Not just because it has so few houses along its short length or because of its location between

Whitehall and St James's Park, but due to the fact that its only residents are chosen from the elected government. Numbers 10 and 11 Downing Street are the official London homes of the Prime Minister and the Chancellor of the Exchequer, the 1st and 2nd Lords of the Treasury, whilst Numbers 9 and 12 provide office accommodation for their key staff and colleagues in government.

The black steel gates facing Whitehall at the entrance to Downing Street were placed there in 1989 during the period when Mrs Thatcher was Prime Minister, preventing members of the public approaching 10 Downing Street without official authorisation.

4. Women at War Memorial

In 2005, 60 years after the end of WWII, another memorial was constructed close to the Cenotaph to honor and remember the work of women during war-time, in the military, emergency services, factories, hospitals and farms. Between 1939 and 1945 women did every job imaginable and many that they would not have been allowed to do before the outbreak of war. They made munitions, drove ambulances, buses and trains, grew food, built ships and even went down the coalmines! At the time of

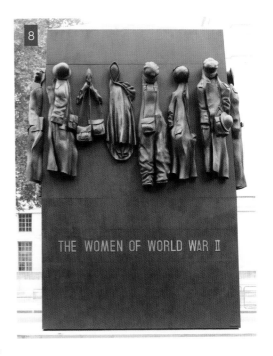

the country's greatest need, women risked their lives to serve their country and many suffered injury or died. This memorial puts women in their proper place in the heart of the nation.

The memorial is a 7 m (23 ft) high bronze sculpture by Essex sculptor, John Mills, and depicts the uniforms and working clothes worn by women during the war.

To fund its installation Baroness Boothroyd (former Speaker of the House of Commons), raised some £800,000 towards the cost of the monument by appearing on the TV show 'Who Wants To Be A Millionaire?' in 2002.

5. The Banqueting House

The Banqueting House at Whitehall was designed by architect Inigo Jones in 1619, and is the only building that remains today of the original Whitehall Palace. Banqueting Houses in the 17th century were traditionally isolated from other palace buildings and this may well account for why the structure was left untouched when the rest of the palace burnt down in 1698. Built in the Palladian style, it was the first of its type in the country with just a single, two-storey double-cube room. King Charles I, a great patron of the arts, commissioned the artist Sir Peter Paul Rubens to decorate the ceiling panels which ironically depict the glorification of his father James I, entitled the 'Apotheosis of James I'. They remain in situ today and are one of Rubens' greatest masterpieces.

Outside the building on a very cold day in late January 1649 King Charles I stood on a scaffold and was executed after having lost his long struggle for power over parliament. As an advocate of the Divine Right of Kings many feared that the king wanted absolute power. Samuel Pepys, the famous 16th century diarist, actually played truant from school in order to witness the event.

Nowadays the building is managed by Historic Royal Palaces and at the time of writing is undergoing restoration. The interior is startling in its simplicity as although named a 'Banqueting House' it contains no kitchens. The building was always used for entertainment alone. Royal receptions, ceremonies and masques (a form of play) were held here, and both Inigo Jones and dramatist and poet Ben Jonson were much involved in the design and construction of sets for these events.

6. Horse Guards, Horse Guards Parade and the Household Cavalry Museum

Horse Guards was built in the Palladian style in the early 1750s, the work of John Vardy and William Kent, and named after the troops who have been the monarch's life guard on the site since the restoration of the monarchy in 1660. Constructed on the site of the Guard House of the old Whitehall Palace, the palace's tilt yard later became the exercise ground of Horse Guards Parade, located directly behind the Horse Guards building. Before Trafalgar Square was developed in 1841, The Mall was closed off at both ends and Horse Guards was the only entrance to both Buckingham Palace and St James's Palace. It remains the 'formal' entrance to both and only the Queen drives through it!

Initially Headquarters for the British Army's general staff, the building served as the offices of the Commander-in-Chief of the British Army and the Duke of Wellington was based here whilst he carried out this role. Since the early 20th century it has been the headquarters of two major Army commands: the London District and the Household Cavalry.

The Horse Guards building is always guarded by troops of the Household Cavalry, (either the Lifeguards in red, or the Blues and Royals in blue) both mounted and on foot and you will see two mounted cavalry troopers posted outside daily between 10am and 4pm, (relieved hourly). A Changing of the Guard ceremony takes place each day at 10.30am (Monday-Saturday) and at 9.30am on Sunday, which is generally less busy than the guard change ceremony outside Buckingham Palace and you will probably be closer to the action!

If you are visiting in mid-September you might catch a guided tour of the building when it opens its doors on the London Open House weekend.

Horse Guards Parade

Horse Guards Parade, sited at the centre of London's ceremonial life and government district is central London's largest open space. In June each year it is the setting for the impressive ceremony of Trooping the Color held on Her Majesty's official birthday by the Queen's personal troops, and for Beating the Retreat military ceremony.

The present Parade Ground was built in the 1740s and replaced a waterway that had previously run through St James's Park. In earlier times the area had been used as a tilt-yard where tournaments were held at King Henry VIII's court and was the setting for Queen Elizabeth I's annual birthday celebrations. Interestingly, throughout much of the 20th century the space was used as a car park for senior civil servants – a far cry from its original purpose!

During the 2012 London Olympic Games the space took on yet another use; this time as the venue for Beach Volleyball! The area was transformed overnight with temporary courts and seating installed, one of which had a capacity for a crowd of 15,000.

Household Cavalry Museum

The museum is located within the Horse Guards building facing the Parade Ground and charts the everyday work of the Household Cavalry, both its ceremonial role and as an operational regiment serving across the globe.

A small but fascinating museum it offers an insight into the troopers' training and tells their personal stories. Horse lovers will delight in seeing the troopers and horses in the on-site 18th century stables. Look at *www.householdcavalrymuseum.co.uk* for further details about the museum.

7. St James's Park

One of eight London Royal Parks, St James's Park is probably the most akin to gardens. At 93 acres it is certainly much smaller than either Hyde Park or The Regent's Park. The park, which owes its name to a former women's leper hospital that had been dedicated to St James was first turned into an area for deer hunting by King Henry VIII in 1532. Subsequently, King James I developed it into a park with formal gardens, an aviary, a menagerie as well as a physic garden. There is even a story that an elephant drank a gallon of wine here every day!

It was from St James's Palace on the edge of the park that King Charles I took his last walk to the Banqueting House in January 1649 before his execution. His father, King Charles II, opened the park to the public and it became a very fashionable resort, a place for Londoners to stroll and meet. It also had its seedier side attracting prostitutes, thieves and duels and it subsequently became illegal to draw a sword within its boundaries.

When King George IV came to the throne in the 1820s he commissioned John Nash to re-plan the canal in the centre of the park as a lake and to re-plant the surroundings in the 'Picturesque' mode and the style remains to this day.

The Park is considered by many to be the most attractive in London and is especially loved for its wildfowl (more than 30 species) which seem to dominate the lake. You can see Canaletto's famous painting of it in Tate Britain at Millbank.

It remains one of London's most popular royal parks and is used by office workers, government officials, and tourists alike, all of whom take delight in its elegant avenues and architecture, its wildlife, the wonderful views and beautiful gardens. It is hardly surprising then that St James's Park is seen in a good number of films. A walk in St James's is central to *Mrs Henderson Presents* (2005); A chase, rather than a walk, through St James's is a high-point of the live action version of *101 Dalmatians* (1996), starring Glenn Close. In the 2002 Bond film, *Die another Day*, starring Pierce Brosnan, the villain Gustav Graves, literally drops into the park parachuting over the Victoria Memorial and into Buckingham Palace on the way to collect his knighthood from the Queen.

8. The Mall: Joint Memorial to George VI and Queen Elizabeth the Queen Mother

Here are two charming bronze memorials to the Queen's parents, King George VI and Queen Elizabeth the Queen Mother. The King is shown in his uniform of an Admiral of the fleet wearing his Garter mantel, whilst his consort, is also draped in Garter robes and depicted at the age she was when the king died in 1952.

What is particularly engaging about the memorial is the addition of bronze reliefs on either side of the Queen Mother which display events and activities of her life. Paul Day, the sculptor, is also responsible for similar works: the Battle of Britain Memorial on the Victoria Embankment and the sculpted frieze on the base of the 'Meeting Place' statue at St Pancras Railway Station.

9. St James's Palace

Today the role of St James's Palace is as the administration centre for the monarchy and High Commissioners present letters, whilst Ambassadors are formally accredited to the Court of St James. Although St James's Palace is the official residence of the sovereign, Buckingham Palace is the monarch's actual London home. Much survives of the redbrick building erected by Henry VIII, including the Chapel Royal, the gatehouse, some turrets and two surviving Tudor rooms in the State apartments. Buildings later sprawled to cover the area of four courts now known as Ambassadors' Court, Engine Court, Friary Court and Color Court. The great Tudor Gatehouse at the southern end of St. James's Street still bears Henry VIII's royal cypher HR, surmounted by his crown. The Palace has a long and interesting history. It was here in 1558 that Mary Tudor signed the treaty surrendering Calais and Queen Elizabeth I set out from St James's in 1588 to address her troops assembled at Tilbury, who were preparing to stave off the expected invasion by the Spanish Armada. Many of the Stuart sovereigns were born at the Palace including the future Charles II and James II, Mary II and Queen Anne. After the destruction of the Palace of Whitehall in 1689 St. James's Palace became the official residence of the monarch until Queen Victoria decided to make Buckingham Palace her official London residence in 1837. After the death of Diana, Princess of Wales, St James's Palace became the home to His Royal Highness (HRH) Prince Charles and his sons, Prince William and Prince Harry until they moved next door to Clarence House in 2003 (following the death of the Queen Mother who had lived there previously).

You have now reached the end of the walk. If you cross the Mall you will find refreshment and toilet facilities just inside St James's Park on the right hand side.

BUCKINGHAM PALACE

(www.royalcollection.org.uk)

Buckingham Palace is easily recognizable by its magnificent iron and gilded bronze gates and railings as well as its central balcony where Her Majesty (HM) The Queen and the Royal Family can be seen on special memorable occasions, such as Jubilee celebrations, and the wedding of Prince William to Catherine Middleton.

At such times the entire Mall and the area in front of Buckingham Palace by the Victoria Memorial are simply heaving with crowds of people and the atmosphere is electric!

The original house was built in the 1700s as a country residence for the Duke of Buckingham situated amongst meadows and streams on the edge of London. Purchased by King George III in 1761 it was the birthplace of 14 of his 15 children and became a real family home. It has however undergone much alteration since, having been enlarged and lavishly decorated and now has 775 rooms, of which 19 are State Rooms.

If you are visiting London between late July and September you will have the opportunity to go inside both Buckingham Palace and its gardens whilst HM The Queen moves to her summer residence at Balmoral in Scotland. The Palace has only opened its doors since 1993 after a devastating fire broke out at Windsor Castle and the Queen wanted to raise money for the ensuing restoration work.

The tour of the palace is primarily around the exquisite State Rooms. These are the public working rooms where sovereigns formally meet, reward, and entertain both their subjects and visiting royalty, and heads of government, whether it be a state, official or ceremonial event.

Much of the décor and artworks came to the Palace from the former Carlton House (since demolished) which had been the London home of King George IV when he was Prince of Wales acting as the Prince Regent. You will see priceless works of art and furniture as well as porcelain and sculpture, all part of the Royal Collection which is held by the monarch in perpetuity on behalf of the nation. The display of art in the 47 m long Picture Gallery is simply amazing with paintings of many famous artists and grand masters including works, amongst others, by Rubens, Titian and Van Dyck.

The Queen and the Royal Family will host dinners and receptions in this gallery and subjects fortunate enough to be receiving an honor will gather here prior to their investiture ceremony held in the splendid and vast Ballroom, the largest and most versatile room in the Palace. Used for banquets, concerts and balls, it was opened in 1856 to celebrate the end of the Crimean War.

A bonus of the tour is the visit to part of the palace gardens, beautifully cared for and full of exotic plants and trees as well as a very lovely lake. The garden forms the exit to the palace visit and there are benches to sit on and admire the views and enjoy the setting. The gardens extend over a 40-acre area and it is here that the Queen's Garden Parties are held throughout the summer months. Public concerts were held here for the first time in 2002 to celebrate the Queen's Golden Jubilee and again the grounds were used in 2006 for a Children's Party at the Palace in the course of the Queen's 80th birthday celebrations.

THE QUEEN'S GALLERY AND ROYAL MEWS

You can visit both attractions on a joint ticket or individually depending on your interest.

Queen's Gallery: Right beside Buckingham Palace is this treasure of a gallery which opened in the 1960s. The idea was to display objects belonging to the Royal Collection through changing exhibitions. With more than a million items the Royal Collection truly reflects the interests and tastes of kings and queens over the past five hundred years, since the restoration of the monarchy in 1660.

It contains paintings, drawings, watercolors, furniture, ceramics, silver, sculpture, jewellery, clocks, books and manuscripts, arms and armour, fans and textiles. The Royal patrons chiefly associated with it are Frederick, Prince of Wales, George III and George IV, Queen Victoria and Prince Albert and Queen Mary, consort of

George V. The Collection is regarded as one of the finest in the world and is significant not only on account of its size but also because it is one of the last great European royal collections still intact.

The Gallery opens daily but closes for a month in the autumn (check website, *www.royalcollection.org.uk* for details) and an admission charge is made.

Only a few meters away you arrive at the **Royal Mews.** Certainly, if you enjoy pageantry and horses the Royal Mews should be included in your itinerary for it is here that you will see some of the carriage horses used on ceremonial occasions as well as the magnificent carriages and coaches employed at these times. In addition, the Royal Mews is home to the State Limousines used by the Royal Family for transport on their official duties. There are two Bentleys, three Rolls Royces and three Daimlers plus several VW people carriers.

William Chambers' Riding House, the oldest building on the site (1765) is still used daily and 34 carriage horses, Cleveland Bays and Windsor Greys, are stabled on site. These are often seen pulling the royal carriages on State Visits, Royal Weddings, the State Opening of Parliament and at the annual Lord Mayor's Show.

One of the most striking and opulent of the coaches here is the Gold State Coach used at every coronation since that of King George IV in 1821. Just added to the collection is the Diamond Jubilee State Coach, a state-of-the-art coach, on display in its own room. This was built to celebrate HM the Queen's Diamond Jubilee in 2012 and is remarkably modern with air conditioning and heating inside. On its roof is an oak carved imperial crown within which is a small camera inserted to allow for filming of the crowds that gather along the route during processional events.

Other carriages to look our for are the 1902 State Landau used by the Duke and Duchess of Cambridge after their wedding ceremony in April 2011, the Australia State Coach (presented to HM The Queen in 1988 marking Australia's bicentenary) and the Glass State Coach (1881), used for Royal Weddings such as that of His Royal Highness (HRH) The Prince of Wales to Lady Diana Spencer in 1981 where it was found to be a little small to contain both the bride and her wedding train!

The Irish State Coach and Queen Alexandra's State Coach are possibly the two most familiar of the collection. The Queen will ride to the State Opening of Parliament in the former whilst the latter transports the Imperial State Crown to Parliament which she will wear at the Opening Ceremony.

To conclude your visit you may want to browse in the excellent Royal Mews shop that leads out to the exit. Once on Buckingham Palace Road you are surrounded by many cafes, restaurants, and pubs and there is an area of shops nearby on Victoria Street. Victoria Underground Station with good connections to central London is only a few minutes walk away.

PICTURE CAPTIONS

1 - Sir Winston Churchill, Parliament Square

2 - Big Ben, The Elizabeth Tower, and the Palace of Westminster

3 - Nelson Mandela, Parliament Square

4 - Soldiers of the Household Division

5 - The State Opening of Parliament Procession 2013

6 - Westminster Abbey, West Front

7 - Clock face of Elizabeth Tower, aka Big Ben

8 - Women of World War II Memorial, Sculptor: John Mills

9 - Horse Guards Parade

10 - Joint Memorial to King George VI and Queen Elizabeth the Queen Mother

11 - The Glass Coach, the Royal Mews

DAY 2

ENTERTAINMENT AND CULTURE IN LONDON'S WEST END

SECTION ONE

TOURIST LONDON

COVENT GARDEN

Today, one of London's major tourist attractions, Covent Garden was originally a garden for the monks at Westminster Abbey (11–16th centuries), the name 'Covent' being a derivation of 'convent'. It was here that food was grown for use by the monastic community based in Westminster, and surprisingly, throughout the intervening years the food association has remained. Market stalls were plying their trade in the central piazza from the middle of the 17th century and then the space developed into a successful fruit, vegetable and flower market. This lasted until the 1970s when the site outlived its purpose, and like Billingsgate Market in the City of London, it relocated out of central London.

Despite the subsequent threat of redevelopment into residential and hotel use, plans were thwarted and Covent Garden with its **Apple Market and Flower Markets** was turned in to a thriving arts and crafts market with small independent shops and stalls and a centre for cuisine with every possible type of food on offer.

Come here now and the area buzzes all day long and well into the early hours of the morning. It is very easy to lose hours here mooching around the shops and market stalls, enjoying the street entertainment, and listening to opera students and singers inside the Apple Market. Or you may choose to while away time in the amazingly well-stocked travel bookshop **Stanfords** or in the enormous **Apple Store** that dominates one side of the square.

When the piazza was developed for the 4th Earl of Bedford in the 1630s he asked his architect, Inigo Jones, to build a chapel to complete the project but stressed that he wanted nothing too expensive, 'nothing much better than a barn'. **St Paul's Church** is what Jones built for him, which he described as 'the handsomest barn in England'. It is indeed a fine church known as the 'Actor's Church', as many in that trade have been interred within its precincts or have memorial plaques on the church walls. As Covent Garden is very close to London's theaterland many actors live and or work in the area and it is here that memorial services are frequently held for people from the acting, writing and media professions.

You are likely to recognize many of the famous names remembered within St Paul's Church from Charlie Chaplin to Vivien Leigh, Noel Coward, Boris Karloff, and Hattie Jacques renowned for her roles in the 'Carry On' films.

The portico of the church is where Professor Higgins met Eliza Doolittle in the 1960s film *My Fair Lady* starring Audrey Hepburn and Rex Harrison. It was also where, three hundred years earlier, the first ever Punch and Judy show was seen in England, witnessed and recorded by the famous diarist, Samuel Pepys in May 1662. Look on the church wall and you will see an inscription logging the event!

In the south-east corner of the piazza based in what was once the Flower Market, is the London Transport Museum. Children love this place and enjoy clambering into mock-up tube carriages and old buses and trams. The museum has a really varied and wide-ranging collection of London's vehicles since the 1800s and is a good place to shop for souvenirs or to grab a coffee.

Close by is the Royal Opera House, home to both the Opera and Royal Ballet. It underwent an enormous redevelopment programme at the end of the 1990s and has transformed both the building and its facilities. For a superb view over the piazza take the escalator up to the top floor roof terrace where you will also find a bar and restaurant.

If time permits wander through the narrow surrounding streets into Neal's Yard, a lovely enclave full of restaurants, fashion shops and even its own 'fringe' theater, the 'Donmar Warehouse'. All the buildings and storerooms here were once associated with the market and you can still see the traces of their original usage, with hoists jutting out from the upper floors where goods and produce were kept before distribution.

Continue a little further north and you reach a roundabout with a central obelisk sundial column. This is Seven Dials, a most vibrant and eclectic neighbourhood just on the edge of London's theaterland. The area was laid out in the early 18th century during the reign of the joint monarchs, William III and Mary II and still has a similar appearance, with its central circus and seven radiating roads. Originally conceived as a residential suburb for wealthy tradesmen, lawyers and gentlemen, in time its houses were converted into shops, lodgings and factories and became more of a working neighbourhood full of watch repairers, wood carvers, booksellers and breweries. Nowadays it is characterized mainly by its

quirky shops, cool, trendy bars, restaurants, hotels, cafes and pubs as well as the Cambridge Theater on the corner of Earlham Street.

Now, walk directly across the circus along the other half of Earlham Street with its small street market, into Shaftesbury Avenue. Here, you turn left into Cambridge Circus. Dominating the west side of the junction is the grand, terracotta faced Palace Theater commissioned by Richard D'Oyly Carte in the late 1880s to be the home of English grand opera. Unable to make a success of the venture he sold the theater within a year of it opening and after a brief spell as the Palace Theater of Varieties, it changed its name in 1911 to the Palace Theater and concentrated on musical productions. This association continues today and the theater has become particularly known for its blockbuster, long-running musicals, such as Les Miserables, and Jesus Christ Superstar. The interior of the theater is just as spectacular as its exterior and is adorned with fabulous Italian marble, chandeliers and onyx and marble panelling.

Cross the Circus, keeping the theater on your right, and continue along the street. At this end of Shaftesbury Avenue there is little to alert you to the fact that you are right in the middle of London's theater district, but as you progress along the street you will see four theaters ahead on the right hand side (the Lyric, Gielgud, Apollo and Queen's). If you take any of the turnings on the right you will find yourself in Soho.

SOHO

Famous as London's red-light district it is also a hub for music and media, theater and the gay scene. As such it is a wonderfully cosmopolitan and frenetic central London village. Its narrow streets are jam-packed with coffee houses, pubs, clubs, eateries of every description, as well as international specialist shops and clubs. Be sure to visit the Algerian Coffee Stores and Gerry's Wine and Spirits on Old Compton Street, both real Aladdin's Caves, and Ronnie

Scott's Jazz Club on Frith Street.

It is still both exciting and a little seedy. From the 17th century on, the area was home to many immigrants; French Huguenots, (expelled from France following the repudiation of the Edict of Nantes in 1685), Italians, Jews and Greeks. The latter subsequently gave its name to one of Soho's main streets, and each group of immigrants undoubtedly contributed to the character of the area. Old Compton Street is regarded as Soho's high street and is full of food and retail outlets, but this can be said for most of the streets that run off it too: Dean Street, Frith Street, Greek Street – you will certainly not go hungry around here!

It was in Dean Street that an impoverished Karl Marx lived with his family in the 1850s and which since the 1920s has been the site of the popular Soho restaurant and private club, Quo Vadis. A plaque on the wall outside No. 28 records him living there and the building itself was given listed status in 1970 largely on account of its association with Marx. A little further along the street is the Soho Theater which has rapidly put itself on the map since its establishment in 2000. The theater specializes in fringe, comedy and cabaret showcasing in particular the work of new writers and stand up comics. It is a really lively cultural centre with two theaters and a cabaret space, and is a great late night venue.

During the 1930s the Black Cat Café on Old Compton Street was where rent boys gathered. Quentin Crisp (author of 'The Naked Civil Servant') was one of their number, and later became a male model at art schools, easily recognized for his hennaed hair and velvet suits. By the 1950s the street was renowned for its coffee bars and clubs: Act One, Scene One was very popular with celebrities from the film and theater industries and the 2i's, became the birthplace of British Rock and Roll.

Naturally, the area appeals largely for its bohemianism but it also has a great deal of history. **Soho Square**, once a royal hunting ground, was established in open fields in the 1680s and its houses immediately attracted the aristocracy. When they moved out, French Huguenots settled here, the first of many waves of immigrants to live in Soho. During the next century it became a fashionable area for ambassadors and later, scientists to live.

As you walk around the pretty leafy square you will notice both the impressive terracotta French Protestant Church in the north-west corner, and St Patrick's Church, Italianate in style, to the east (that serves both the Irish and Italian communities). Both churches were established in the last years of the 19th century and are much in use today reflecting the nature of the area.

Soho nowadays is considered to be very much at the heart of publishing, the media and music industries so it is not surprising to find the offices of the British Board of Film Classification at no. 3, at no.31–32 are the 20th Century Fox Film Co. and Paul McCartney's London offices for MPL Communications Ltd are at No 1.

Interestingly, the district is also renowned for its connection with the medical profession and health services. John Hunter (who transformed surgery) and his brother, William (responsible for establishing the first anatomy school), moved here in the 18th century, and later three specialist hospitals were set up treating skin diseases and 'diseases of women'. Physician John Snow identified the source of a cholera outbreak in Soho in 1854 to a public water pump in Broadwick Street, and this subsequently revolutionized the water and waste systems of London and the betterment of public health globally. Queen Victoria also benefited from his discoveries, taking chloroform administered by Snow when giving birth to two of her children.

So, like Covent Garden, there is plenty to see and do in Soho whether you visit to admire its architecture, sample its cuisine and pubs or arrive after dark when the club and bar scene gets going.

PICCADILLY CIRCUS, LEICESTER SQUARE, CHINATOWN AND TRAFALGAR SQUARE

Moments after leaving Soho you will arrive in Piccadilly Circus, equally busy, and included in every itinerary of London. Really it is just a traffic junction of 5 roads in the middle of which stands the winged naked aluminium statue 'Eros', the God of Love. Like Times Square in New York City, Piccadilly Circus is a wonderful place to come for the atmosphere alone, and cannot be beaten for people watching. It is also a most centrally sited, easily accessible location to meet up with friends. Its dazzling neon signs light up the entire area both during the day and at night, and the place teems with people: shoppers from Regent Street and Oxford Street, theater goers from Shaftesbury Avenue and visitors from every country of the world!

Walk slightly east, past the London Trocadero and you arrive in Leicester Square, home to London's major cinemas. This is where film premieres are held, the red carpet laid down and many celebrities, actors, and even members of the Royal Family come. You'll need to get to the square early on premiere evenings if you want to have a chance of seeing the stars close up as Leicester Square is always swarming with hordes of people and any event in the area just makes it all the busier.

Whatever time of the year you visit you will find events taking place within the square's gardens, sometimes to complement a UK film premiere, whilst at other times there will be a festival, music or some other activity in full swing.

On the south side by the Leicester Square Clock Tower is the Discount Ticket Booth, TKTS, and is the official place to pick up cheap and bargain tickets for same-day performances of shows and plays. Often you may pay as little as half the original ticket price, and manage to sit in good seats too. The ticket booth opens Monday-Saturday 10am-7pm, and Sunday 11am-4.30pm, and a small booking fee is charged for the service. Payment can be made on card (Visa, Mastercard and UK Maestro), using cash, theater tokens or certain vouchers, but not with travelers or bank cheques or American Express.

The imposing black granite art-deco Odeon cinema to the east of the square began its life as a theater in 1868 and it was here that the debut of the 'Can-Can' was performed. The dance was then considered an outrage resulting in the theater losing its licence for some years. Demolished in the 1930s it was later re-built as a cinema becoming the Odeon chain's front-runner, and the scene of numerous film premieres since.

Chinatown

On the northern edge of Leicester Square behind the M&M's World store and Empire Cinema you find yourself in an almost entirely different environment, Chinatown. The Chinese established themselves here from the 1970s when the community moved from the Docklands of East London. War-time bombing was the impetus as many of their homes and businesses had been destroyed or badly damaged. This area, that was fairly run-down and squalid post WWII was offering cheap rents and Chinese entrepreneurs were able to pick up short-term leases at a very good price. It was also a period of immigration by Hong Kong farm workers, which greatly boosted the numbers of the Chinese community living in London.

Over the years Chinatown has grown significantly and now extends from Shaftesbury Avenue in the north to Leicester Square in the south and is bounded by Wardour Street in the west and Charing Cross Road to the east. The area is crammed with restaurants (mainly specializing in Cantonese cuisine), grocers, bakeries, herbalists and Chinese supermarkets, a delight to visit as they sell all manner of exotic foods and spices. Eating in one of the restaurants is highly recommended and there is no shortage of choice. Whatever your budget or taste you are sure to find something to suit, and it will definitely be a memorable occasion.

If you are visiting during the Chinese New Year join the wonderful and very colorful celebrations in Gerrard Street and its neighbourhood. With lion and dragon dances, streets full of entertainment, lanterns swaying and firework displays it must be the best time to experience a bit of China. Gerrard Street is easily recognizable by its large Chinese gates, street furniture and stone lions as well as a Chinese pagoda! Its street signs are written in Mandarin as well as English marking the area it encompasses.

Trafalgar Square

Like Piccadilly Circus, Trafalgar Square is another hub, always lively and full of

people and activity. Adorned with statues of British monarchs and military figures and dominated by Nelson's Column (commemorating his naval victory over Napoleon at the Battle of Trafalgar) the Square has always been a place where people gather for rallies, demonstrations, festivals and New Year's Eve celebrations.

Cultural events frequently

take place in the Square: opera is relayed on big screens, religious festivals are celebrated, dancing acts and performances from the Far East and Africa are staged, as well as events like the Malaysian Night Market and the Russian Maslenitsa, a sun festival celebrating the end of winter.

At Christmas time the Square is the focus for carol-singing around the massive and beautifully lit Christmas tree, an annual gift from the people of Norway in gratitude for Britain's support during World War Two.

Throughout the year visitors come to this landmark attraction enjoying its position and space in the very centre of London, participating in its many festivals, and simply taking delight in the square itself with its attractive fountains and giant bronze lions at the foot of Nelson's Column. There is a café, lift and toilets by the flight of steps leading up to the National Gallery perched above the Square. Climb the staircase to get a really good view to the south of Whitehall, home to many government departments, the Palace of Westminster and Big Ben, as well as Admiralty Arch to the west and of St Martins-in-the-Fields, the beautiful Greek Revival style church to the east. The church is renowned for its music and many recitals and concerts are held here, some of which are free.

Two unusual features of the Square are the tiny police box in the south-east corner, now used for storage, and the 4th Plinth, in the north-west corner, which until 1999 had laid empty for many years. Since then however, the plinth has been used to highlight contemporary works of art and a number of noted artists have provided works for it. Always controversial, the art displayed has been most diverse ranging from Yinka Shonibare's 'Nelson's Ship in a Bottle', Marc Quinn's 'Alison Lapper Pregnant' to Katharina Fritsch's 'Hahn/Cock'. The current 2015 commission 'Gift Horse' by Hans Haacke is of a skeleton horse and is based on an etching by the British artist George Stubbs whose art is on display in the National Gallery immediately behind the plinth.

DAY TRIPS FROM CENTRAL LONDON

HAMPTON COURT PALACE

A visit to Hampton Court is certainly very special as it is actually two Royal palaces in one: Tudor (16th century) and Baroque (end 17th/early 18th century) with the most magnificent buildings and gardens. It has great associations with royalty and in particular, Henry VIII and his wives and was home to the Georgian Court until 1737. In later years lodgings were provided here to Grace and Favour residents (those who had made a vital contribution to their country), including arctic explorer Sir Robert Falcon-Scott, Lady Baden-Powell of the Guiding and Scouting Movement, and scientist Professor Michael Faraday.

The palace is easily accessible and can be reached by road, rail and boat from central London and is surrounded by beautiful parkland, water and gardens. It is easy to spend an entire day here as there is so much to see and do. Children will love the family trails all about Palace ghosts, as well as the enthralling maze, with its network of blind alleys and over 2 m (6.5 ft) high hedges. There are also the Time Explorers interactive adventures for children aged 7–11 guaranteed to keep them busy. Adults can tour the palace using an audio guide (available in a number of languages) or take a private tour with one of Hampton Court Palace's qualified tourist guides.

In addition to the magnificent Tudor Kitchens and State Rooms, there are also the State Apartments of William III, the Chapel Royal and the recently discovered Georgian chocolate kitchen. Andrea Mantegna's series of paintings, the Triumphs of Caesar, possibly some of the most significant Italian Renaissance paintings in the world, are housed beside the Lower Orangery Garden and are a real treat for art lovers, as is the Cumberland Art Gallery with its stunning collection of paintings from the Royal Collection.

Outside in the extensive grounds you can visit the old Great Vine, (almost 250 years old) the Privy, Pond, Knot and King's Kitchen gardens, and enjoy Home Park with its wide spaces and stock of fallow deer.

Two of the palace's most popular events are the annual musical festival in June and the RHS Flower Show in July. If Hampton Court appears familiar this may be because it was the venue for the Cycling Time Trials Event during the London 2012 Olympics and was also where the Olympic Flame began its final journey towards the Olympic Stadium. Torchbearers guided the Flame through the grounds and then on to the river where it was carried to its final London destination.

Oxford and/or Cambridge

Both ancient university towns are about an hour's journey from the centre of London offering wonderful architecture and splendid college campuses. Despite the distance between them they are very similar and the colleges all have a dining hall, quadrangles, student accommodation and teaching rooms. **Oxford**, is the larger, less compact than its counterpart but both are graced with rivers, meadows, and serene surroundings. **Cambridge** is found to the north of

London and is now established as a high technology centre (Silicon Fen) and is greatly involved in the software and bioscience industries. In contrast, Oxford is famed for its motorsport companies, printing and publishing. It is home to the Oxford University Press.

GREENWICH AND GREENWICH PENINSULA

The Greenwich Peninsula is home to the O2 Centre, a major London sports and events arena where the world's top stars perform regularly. Tennis tournaments, international concerts, circus acts, comedy, pop music – are all staged here and up to 20,000 spectators can be seated in the building. In addition, the centre has a cinema, bowling alley, restaurants and bars and for those who like a bit of adventure you can even climb the roof! Not only challenging it is also a wonderful opportunity to gain 360° degree views of Greenwich, Canary Wharf

and the Queen Elizabeth Olympic Park. To discover more about sights within Greenwich refer to Day 3.

WINDSOR CASTLE

Official home to HRH The Queen where she often entertains foreign heads of state and dignitaries. She has her own private apartments but members of the public have access to the state apartments within the castle and into the castle grounds. An imposing fortress built high on an escarpment the castle is most impressive. Nestling above the town and the river Thames below it is a real fairy tale setting. There are many lovely tea-shops, boutiques and interesting shops throughout the town and lovely gardens to stroll in beside the river.

St Albans

Only 25 miles north of London this old Roman town, Verulamium, is easily reached by train from St Pancras using Thameslink rail services. It is very quaint with delightful medieval buildings dating back to the 17th century. A lively and colorful market is held in the town's central market place every Wednesday and Saturday selling everything from fresh fish and meat to clothing, mirrors, handbags, jewellery, hats, candles and food. The Cathedral dominates the town and is well worth a visit. A short walk downhill brings you to the Verulamium Museum, which contains all manner of objects from the Roman period including wonderful house mosaics, coins, a skeleton, jewellery and pottery. Nearby are the remains of the Roman baths with their hypercaust system of underground heating and plunge pools.

Brighton

A mere hour's journey from London by train brings you to Brighton, one of the south coast's jewels. Both a thriving town as well as a seaside resort, Brighton has long been a favourite with Londoners escaping the city and wanting to be beside the sea. It is famous for its piers, the Lanes (alleys full of antique shops) and the Brighton Pavilion, a somewhat unusual looking building of Asian design close to the seafront. Built in the 1820's for the Prince Regent (who later became George IV) it has an exotic Indian looking exterior with minarets and domes, and is full of Chinoiserie inside. Whether you like it or hate it, you have to visit for the experience alone.

SECTION TWO

CULTURAL AND LEGAL LONDON

ROYAL OPERA HOUSE – BACKSTAGE TOUR AND TEA DANCE

The Royal Opera House first appeared on its present site in 1732 and was initially known as the Theater Royal at Covent Garden. In its early years, designated a patent theater, it focused on the spoken word and drama although Handel played at the theater regularly (between 1735–59) and many of his operas and oratorios were written for Covent Garden or had their first London performances there. In the following century the theater staged drama, opera and ballet and sometimes, performances on the high wire by Madame Sacchi, the Italian acrobat. Then, in 1843, the Theaters Act broke the patent theaters' monopoly of drama which had existed for almost 200 years and this enabled Covent Garden to become a venue entirely focused on opera and ballet.

The theater changed its name to the Royal Opera House in 1892 and winter and summer seasons of opera and ballet were given. After closure during the two world wars, the theater re-opened in 1946 and before long it became home to both the Royal Ballet and Royal Opera. The present Royal Opera House (designed by Jeremy Dixon with Bill Jack of Building Design Partnership, BDP), was re-built between 1996–9 with a capacity of over 2,200. In three years the most inadequate of the great opera houses of the world was transformed, not only for audiences, but equally for performers and its employees.

You may have taken a peek inside the Royal Opera House on your previous visit or even attended a performance here, but a tour around the building and behind the scenes is really special, and may be something you either didn't know about or hadn't considered before.

Backstage tours cover the exciting history of the theater and its recent transformation, taking you both backstage and into the front of house areas.

Sometimes you will be lucky enough to see the Royal Ballet rehearsing or even see how the backstage equipment is used. No two tours are the same and will depend much upon what is going on within the Opera House on the day you visit.

Should you be more interested in architecture, the Opera House also runs a 'Velvet, Gilt and Glamour' tour. Taking place at 4pm and slightly shorter than the Backstage Tour it lasts 45 minutes, and concentrates on the auditorium itself and its design, and you will also hear about famous opera singers who have performed at Covent Garden.

In the case of either tour it is best to book on-line in advance of your trip.

You can conclude your visit by enjoying a glass of champagne or by taking afternoon tea in the Paul Hamlyn Hall. Alternatively, visit the Amphitheater Restaurant and Terrace at the top of the building for wonderful views over the Covent Garden piazza below.

Once a month **Tea Dances** are held in the Paul Hamlyn Hall as a reminder of when the Royal Opera House was one of London's great dance venues during WWII. Lasting a couple of hours you can dance to the music of the Royal Opera Dance Band; Tango or waltz the afternoon away or try out your quickstep! See the Opera House website (*www.roh.org.uk*) for details.

THE BRITISH MUSEUM

This is a place where you could spend many hours or even days as its collections are so vast. With artifacts from every continent and from pre-historic times, the British Museum contains the history and culture of ancient civilizations and is truly international in character.

Established in 1753 it owes much of its original collection to a royal physician, Hans Sloane, who had worked and lived in Jamaica. Just before he died he sold his collection to the government for £20,000, the money for which was raised via a national lottery, and the exhibits have been displayed on this site from that time.

Other significant collections have been added in the intervening years and the Museum today is known for the variety of its exhibits as well as the breadth of their range. It is particularly famous for its Egyptian galleries, the Rosetta Stone, Oriental and Middle Eastern Art, Greek and Roman sculptures, treasures from Roman Britain and the Saxon and Viking eras. But these are just a fraction of the objects held in the Museum and available to view. There are ceramic pots from Africa, South American carvings, Oriental religious statues, coins, clocks. The list is endless.

Free 'eye-opener' and 'spot-light' tours are given throughout the day as well as an excellent 'Highlights' tour (charged). The museum stays open until 6pm on weekdays, but on Fridays until 8.30pm and admission is free (except for special exhibitions).

A convenient place to begin your visit is in the Great Court, a wonderful space covered by a glass roof added to the museum in December 2000. Here you can pick up a Museum map at the Information Desk to help orientate yourself. With about 2-3 hours to spare I would suggest the following route:

1. Room 1: Enlightenment Gallery

This charts the era when the British Museum became established (1680–1820) and a visit here is a good way to understand the Museum and acquaint yourself with its collections. Its many objects demonstrate how collectors of the time considered and categorized the treasures and artworks from the world they explored and is an ideal overview of the museum as a whole and excellent starting off point.

In this room you will see a copy of the Rosetta Stone which you are free to approach and even touch, getting a feel for its shape and size. This is a wonderful indulgence as the real stone is displayed behind glass in Room 4, prohibiting you from handling it in any way.

2. Room 4: The Rosetta Stone

has been displayed in the British Museum since 1802, having been discovered by Napoleon's soldiers at el-Rashid (Rosetta) in 1799 and later ceded to the British King, George III under the terms of the Treaty of Alexandria. The importance of the Rosetta Stone was that it contained the script of three languages in separate sections: Ancient Greek at the bottom, Egyptian demotic in the middle and hieroglyphics at the top. The latter had been a lost language for about 1400 years. When it became clear that the first two sections were identical in meaning the stone's significance was realized and became the key to unlocking the code of hieroglyphics. Even so, it took many years before scholars were able to wholly decipher the language, mainly the work of an English physicist, Thomas Young, and a Frenchman, Jean-Francois Champollion.

3. Room 23: The Assyrian Gateway Figures

Here you have a set of magnificent figures, human-headed winged bulls which date to circa 710BC. They arrived in the museum in the mid-19th century coming from Khorsabad in Assyria. Originally, used to guard entrances to palace buildings to ward off evil, to awe visitors and protect the king, they are indeed very impressive. Walk round the figures and count the number of legs, unusually 5 in total, 4 visible at the side and 2 visible at the front! Also see their horned caps and ropes, the signs of divinity and protective spirits.

4. Room 18: The Parthenon Sculptures

These iconic and splendid sculptures dating from the 5th century BC must be included in any tour of the museum for their amazing craftsmanship and beauty. Here within the Duveen Gallery you find the pediment statues at either end of the long room as well as the marble Parthenon frieze containing the story of the four yearly festival celebrating the goddess Athena's birthday by the people of Athens. The wonderful attention to detail on the pediment statues, the folds of the clothing, realistic bodies and feeling of movement is astonishing on work of such an age. Likewise, the portrayal of the horses and gods on the marble frieze are wonderfully life-like.

Re-trace your steps back to Room 4 to see:

5. Room 4: Egyptian Sculpture Room

Immediately in front of you is the 2-toned granite giant bust of Rameses the Great (a pharaoh of the 19th Dynasty, 13th century BC), which was originally located in the Ramesseum, his mortuary temple at Thebes, present day Luxor. Initially part of a pair of enormous seated figures the statue must have fallen down and because of its weight (over seven tons), left there. Look closely and you see a hole on the right hand side which is said to have been made when an unsuccessful attempt was made to move it by the members of Napoleon's expedition in Egypt at the end of the 1700s. It was not until 1816 that the bust was finally moved employing traditional techniques such as poles, ropes and rollers, the same equipment that the workers had used centuries earlier!

When it arrived at the museum two years later it met with great acclaim and was said to have inspired the British poet, Percy Bysshe Shelley to write his poem, Ozymandias.

Walk through gallery to the end and climb the stairs up to the 1st floor. Turn left and make your way to:

6. Rooms 61-64: Egyptian mummies

In this suite of rooms you find not only mummies but also the equipment used to mummify bodies in ancient Egypt, richly colored coffins, canopic jars and even some mummified animals including a small bull, birds and cats. These rooms are some of the most popular in the Museum and may at times be very busy but it is worth persevering and staying a while as there is much to look at and to discover about the burials of ancient Egypt. There are many interesting objects as well as a good deal of information about the practice of mummification.

7. Room 64: Gebelein Man

In **Room 64** you will see a glass cabinet containing the remains of a 5000 year old man, **Gebelein Man**. Nicknamed 'Ginger' on account of the color of his hair, it is a wonderful example of a sand/desert burial where the body has been preserved due to its shallow desert grave. Bacteria was prevented from spreading because the environment absorbed all the body's liquids, and thus the body was left largely intact. Ginger's mummy is lying on its side in the foetal position, common in such burials, and he is surrounded by objects typical of the time he is thought to have died, around 3500 BC.

Exit the room, and pass into Room 65 where you will turn right towards the Roman-British gallery.

8. Room 49: Roman Britain Gallery

First you come to a glass cabinet containing the remains of **Lindow Man.** The remarkably well preserved body displayed was found buried in a peat bog in the north west of England and brought to the British Museum for scientific examination in 1984.

Using radiocarbon dating his death has been established as being between 2BC and AD119 and subsequent research has provided the greatest amount of data about any prehistoric person found in the country. The peat environment allowed for the high degree of preservation of the man's hair and skin as well as many of his internal organs, and scientists investigating the body have been able to establish his age, height, weight and state of health at the time of death. They even know the probable contents of his last meal and how it was cooked! He certainly met an untimely death, having been struck heavily on the head and in the back, suffered a broken neck, and was finally placed face down in the bog. Not a natural death for sure and he may well have been the victim of human sacrifice or a ritual killing.

Further along the gallery on the right within a long glass cabinet you find the **Vindolanda** tablets which are acknowledged as being the oldest British handwritten documents in existence. Vindolanda was a Roman fort in the north of England near Hadrian's Wall and home to soldiers billeted there. The tablets made of very slim slices of wood display personal correspondence as well as military documents, a superb record of life of the period. Due to their fragility only a small number are exhibited and each is really quite fascinating; one is written as a birthday invitation sent by one army officer's wife to another. Not really much different from today!

The Gallery also boasts some exquisite mosaics and Roman hordes of silver buried in fields during the Roman occupation in the 1st-5th centuries AD. The **Mildenhall Treasure** towards the end of the room is an extremely good example of one such treasure trove.

Discovered during WWII in a field in the east of England the horde consists of exquisite silver tableware: dishes, bowls, spoons and ladles, attributed to the late Roman Empire c.360AD because of its style and ornamentation. Stunning objects, they display mythological decoration using engraving and black and silver (niello) inlays. The Great Dish in particular illustrates this having a beautifully engraved surface with small balls soldered all around its edge and adorned with scenes alluding to the worship of Bacchus, the god of wine, on land and sea.

Who owned the horde and why it was buried in the field remains a mystery. Due to its quality it is likely to have been owned by someone of wealth or nobility, but it is hard to imagine anyone abandoning such a set of tableware willingly. Theories abound as to its burial: perhaps it was hurriedly hidden at a time when east England was being attacked by foreign raiders and that something subsequently prevented the owners from reclaiming their collection.

9. Room 41: Sutton Hoo

Very recently re-furbished, this room is dedicated to the treasures of **the Sutton Hoo Ship burial** from Anglo-Saxon England in the 7th century. The objects which are now beautifully displayed in glass cabinets, are a tremendous insight into Anglo-Saxon society and include drinking horns, shoulder clasps, a helmet and even remnants of a lyre.

10. Room 40: Medieval European Gallery

This gallery is packed with many excellent artefacts but there are two in particular that you should not miss!

The first are the **Lewis Chessmen**. These 12th century chess pieces were recovered from the west coast of Scotland in 1831 and it is still a mystery as to their origin. Made of walrus-ivory they are both intricately carved and finely sculpted. By the patterns on the back of the kings they appear to be Scandinavian and it is believed that they might well have come from Norway.

The Museum has 83 of the pieces and also some ivory counters. The lovely chunky pieces are said to be the inspiration for the magic chess set used in J K Rowling's 'Harry Potter' books.

The second, and one of the British Museum's greatest prizes is **The Royal Gold Cup**, an absolutely striking work of art. The cup, manufactured in the 14th century is adorned with punched work, and has vividly painted scenes on its cover, bowl and stand, which record the life and death of St Agnes. Originally made in Paris, the cup passed through a number of hands, was lodged in an Italian convent for almost 400 years, but was ultimately returned to France and sold to the British Museum in the late 19th century.

To conclude your visit you need to pass into **room 36** and then walk down the South Staircase into the main entrance hall. The tour will have shown you a mere fraction of the Museum's collections but will hopefully give you some idea of the wonderful treasures displayed here. An excellent shop is located in the entrance hall, with further shops, café, restaurant and toilet facilities in the Great Court.

INNS OF COURT AND TEMPLE CHURCH

Across the road from the Royal Courts of Justice, down a small alleyway (Devereux Court) you come into an entirely unexpected area, that of the world of lawyers. Located off Fleet Street, t
his area is known as **'The Temple'** which before the 14th century was home to the Knights Templar, an order of powerful Soldier Monks who protected pilgrims on their way to the Holy Land. The Knights took vows of chastity, poverty and obedience and their lives were strictly regulated. In order to do their job they needed to raise funds and recruit men, so they built monasteries in many capitals of Europe. The London Temple was their Headquarters in Britain.

The Order was abolished in 1312 by the Pope and their lands were passed over to the Knights of St John of Jerusalem, but as they already had ample estates they leased the buildings to two colleges of lawyers, namely, Middle and Inner Temple, who gathered at the site due to its proximity to the royal courts nearby at Westminster Hall. Both Inns occupy the same sites today and the buildings form campuses similar to those found in Oxford and Cambridge. Each Inn has its own dining hall, chapel, library, quadrangles, gardens as well as chambers, originally used for accommodation, but now largely in use as barristers' offices.

You are presently standing in the grounds of Middle Temple, easy to recognize through its symbol, the lamb with a staff, which is prominently displayed everywhere: on drainpipes, above doorways, on gates, lamp-posts and railings. Pass through Fountain Court, so named because of its central fountain. According to Shakespeare in his play Henry VI, Part II, the gardens beyond were the venue of a meeting between representatives of the House of York and House of Lancaster and marked the start of the ensuing War of the Roses (1455–1487) when a white rose for the House of York and red rose for the House of Lancaster, were plucked.

These beautiful gardens stretching down to the banks of the Thames are an unexpected quiet haven from the hustle and bustle of London. They open to the public during the working week between 12.30 and 3pm.

Stop by Middle Temple Hall on your right. The Hall, built in Elizabethan times (1562–1573) prides itself on possessing one of the finest double hammer-beam roofs in England which fortunately survived WWII intact. It also has an unusually long 9.5 m (31 ft) 'high table', made up of three planks from a single oak tree grown in Windsor Forest, a gift it is said, from Queen Elizabeth I before the Hall was completed.

Below the table stands a cupboard, believed to have been made from the hatch cover of Sir Francis Drake's ship, the Golden Hinde, in which he circumnavigated the globe. It is on this cupboard that newly qualified barristers sign their  names when they are called to the Bar.

Middle Temple Hall has always been the core of the Inn's life and attracted many famous visitors (such as explorers, Sir Walter Raleigh and Sir Martin Frobisher) as well as members. In the 17th century the renowned diarist John Evelyn was a member of the Inn as was Charles Dickens in the 1800s.

The Hall, then as now, was not only used for dining and training but also for entertainment; plays and pageants were performed here on many occasions. Shakespeare's 'Twelfth Night' had its first ever performance here in 1602, and the tradition of entertainment continues today in the yearly Christmas Revels, written and performed by the Inn's students, barristers and senior members (the Benchers).

On a daily basis, the Hall is open to members of the public in the morning between 9.30am and midday, (weekdays, though not on public holidays) and used by lawyers at lunch-time and in the evenings during the dining terms. Many functions of Middle Temple are held here and additionally, the Hall is hired out as a venue for weddings, receptions, banquets and parties.

Middle Temple Hall, on account of its buildings, grounds, cobbled streets and gas lighting has been regularly used as a film location in movies like *Bridget Jones II- The Edge of Reason, The Good Shepherd, The Wolfman, Shakespeare in Love, Poirot, The Da Vinci Code* as well as BBC television dramas.

From here, walk ahead crossing Middle Temple Lane into Pump Court. Stop for a moment to look at the notice boards listing the names of members of the Chambers. The members are barristers and QC's (Queen's Counsel), the advocates who stand up in court and put a case before a judge and sometimes, though not always, a jury.

At the end of the Court pass through the Cloisters into Inner Temple and Temple Court. **Inner Temple,** can also be easily identified by its emblem, Winged Pegasus, the flying horse. Like Middle Temple's Lamb you will see Pegasus conspicuously hanging on all Inner Temple buildings and furniture.

Temple Court is dominated by the beautiful Temple Church on the north side (left) and Inner Temple Hall on the south (right) and has an imposing column in its centre with a sculpture of two knights on horseback, the work of Nicola Hicks. An ancient image, according to the 13th century monk of St Albans, Matthew Paris, it represents the Knight's lack of horses and humble beginnings.

Temple Church is used as a chapel by both Inner and Middle Temples and is based on the round church of the Holy Sepulchre in Jerusalem. It is a Royal Peculiar with its Master officially appointed by HM The Queen, but she devolves the oversight to the Dean of the Chapel Royals, who is currently the Bishop of London. When attending the church members of Inner Temple sit on the south side, whilst those of Middle Temple sit on the north side.

The Knights Templar built their church in the Gothic style towards the end of the 12th century. It became the Headquarters of the Knights in England and it was here that they worshipped and were buried. King Henry III so liked the church that he intended to be interred here (although he was actually buried in Westminster Abbey) and it is because of this that the church was built in such an elaborate and magnificent style.

Badly damaged in bombing raids during WWII the Church underwent a programme of major restoration in the 1950s at which point a new roof and

choir were added. The acoustics are wonderful and every Wednesday lunchtime an organ recital takes place here.

Following the release of the film, The Da Vinci Code in 2006, Temple Church almost became a place of pilgrimage. Its very beautiful round nave full of effigies of the Knights Templar appeared in the film as the setting for one of the clues that the two heroes of the story, Sophie Neveu and Robert Langdon, had to solve. If you have read the book or seen the movie a visit inside will certainly evoke memories!

Before leaving Inner Temple look to your right where the fairly modern building you see is Inner Temple Hall. It replaced the much older Hall that was destroyed during the 1939-45 War. Like Middle Temple Hall it is used for dining, for functions and events. Generally, it is not open to the public except on the annual London Open House weekend in September when you get

the opportunity to see inside as well as visit Middle Temple Hall, barristers' chambers and the libraries.

Leave Temple Court and now pass under the archway into the cobbled courtyard and make your way towards the eastern Tudor Street gate on the left. Just before you exit, walk about 20 m (65 ft) along King's Bench Walk, the set of terraced buildings by the Gate that extend towards the river. Stop outside Chambers at No 11 Kings Bench Walk and look up at the display of names on the board by the doorway. Here you will see names that you are possibly familiar with, namely that of Tony Blair (Prime Minister 1997–2007), and Lord Irvine of Lairg, Lord Chancellor in Blair's government, and also renowned for having introduced the young Blair to his wife, Cherie when they were both pupil barristers. Lord Irvine actually referred to himself as 'Cupid QC' at their subsequent wedding!

Finally, exit into Tudor Street and walk to the junction with New Bridge Street. You will see Blackfriars underground station ahead of you, served by the Circle and District tube lines. Right next door to it is one of London's great historic pubs, the Blackfriar, renowned for its superbly crafted art-nouveau exterior and interior decoration. Go inside to see the wall mosaics and sculptures many featuring chubby black friars and perhaps stop here for a while to rest your weary feet!

PICTURE CAPTIONS

1 - Covent Garden Piazza

2 - Soho Square

3 - Chinatown

4 - Royal Courts of Justice

5 - Royal Opera House

6 - Royal Opera House, Paul Hamlyn Hall

7 - Great Court, British Museum

8 - Middle Temple Hall

9 - Temple Church

10 - The Blackfriar Pub

DAY 3

HISTORIC LONDON

SECTION ONE

FORTRESS, BRIDGE AND DOCK

THE TOWER OF LONDON

The Tower, officially, Her Majesty's Royal Palace and Fortress, the Tower of London, has existed on this site for almost 1000 years and is a designated UNESCO World Heritage Site. Constructed in the 1070s for William, Duke of Normandy, as a stronghold to defend London the fortress was also built to intimidate its citizens, and has relished a long and multi-purpose history. It is first and foremost a castle with over 20 towers and was built as a palace for kings. Although royalty have not lived here for over 500 years it is still home to the Tower Yeoman Warders (the Beefeaters), The Constable of the Tower and the eight Tower ravens. These birds have lived here for centuries and legend says that if they were to depart the Tower would disintegrate and the kingdom would fall. Look closely at the birds and you will see they have clipped wings ensuring that they cannot escape and making them the Tower's only present-day prisoners!

The Tower from the very start became the symbol of strength and power of the sovereign, used not only as home to the Royal Mint, Observatory and Zoo but also to house the Public Records, the Armoury, Treasury and as a prison for traitors. Over the centuries it became renowned for its royal executions, torture chambers and its entrance from the river, Traitor's Gate. Many stories are told of imprisonment and torture within the Tower but contrary to popular belief there were only seven actual executions carried out on Tower Green within the castle walls. Most hanging and executions took place on Tower Hill outside the fortress in the area today in front of Trinity Square (next to Tower Hill Underground Station) and a memorial has been placed at the spot listing the names of those who lost their lives here.

Try to put aside several hours to get the most from your trip to the Tower as there is much to see and do and an early start is advised if you want to see all the sights before the many tourist groups appear! If you can arrive before the Tower opens at 9am you will see a little of the Tower ceremony when the Duty Yeoman Warder officially opens the massive wooden doors after which visitors are granted entry.

Undoubtedly, a visit to see the Crown Jewels should be your first port of call in order to avoid long queues later in the day. Exhibited in the Jewel House the Crown Jewels on display have been used and worn at coronation ceremonies since the 1660s. They are utterly priceless and contain the magnificent world famous diamonds, Cullinan I and II, extracted in 1905 in South Africa from a huge rough diamond, the largest ever discovered, as well as the Indian Koh-i-Noor diamond set in the crown of the late Queen Elizabeth the Queen Mother for the 1937 Coronation. In addition you will see on display a range of royal regalia such as orbs, sceptres, crowns, coronation spoons, rings, swords, bracelets and robes. As you would expect

the Crown Jewels (generally referred to as 'Regalia'), display the many objects used during the English coronation service as well as ceremonial and symbolic pieces associated with the coronations of kings and queens.

Since much of the early Regalia was melted down and the gemstones sold off during the 17th century Civil War, a whole new set of Regalia had to be made when Charles II was restored to the throne in 1660. This cost almost £13,000, an enormous sum of money at the time. The only pieces remaining from the period before the mid-17th century are the 12th century gold Anointing Spoon which is used during the coronation ceremony to anoint the Sovereign with holy oil, and three coronation swords, all of which are exhibited.

Once you have entered the Jewel House you pass through several rooms before reaching the vault where the coronation regalia and jewels are displayed. If you want to learn more about the objects you are about to see delay your entry into the vault and cross into the area with benches to the right of the vault entrance. Here you have the opportunity to sit and watch the Queen's coronation ceremony in 1953 and see the regalia in use throughout the ceremony.

Then walk through the vault doorway into the room where the precious collection of crowns and coronation regalia is kept. There are two slow-moving walkways on either side of the display cabinets as well as a raised platform above, and you will have an excellent view of the crowns, sceptres and famous jewels from any of these.

Make sure to look out for:

St Edward's Crown – a solid gold crown weighing 2.23 kg (4.9 lbs) and adorned with precious and semi-precious stones. It is placed on the sovereign's head by the Archbishop of Canterbury during the coronation ceremony.

The Imperial State Crown – Worn by the sovereign when leaving Westminster Abbey after the coronation service and regularly for the State Opening of

Parliament this crown contains over 3,000 gemstones. It is extremely ornate and includes the second largest stone cut from the Cullinan Diamond, (the Second Star of Africa), the Black Prince's Ruby as well as Queen Elizabeth's Pearls, the Stuart Sapphire and St Edward's Sapphire.

The Sovereign's Orb, Sceptre with Dove and Sceptre with Cross – The latter displaying the Great Star of Africa which is the largest unblemished, colorless cut diamond known to mankind and weighs 530 carats.

The Crown of Queen Elizabeth the Queen Mother – containing the Koh-i-Noor (Mountain of Light) diamond from India, the most celebrated of all the diamonds in the Jewel House. Given to Queen Victoria in 1850 the diamond is said to bring bad luck to any man who wears it!

Queen Victoria's Crown – a light crown especially made for the Queen in 1870 as a substitute to the heftier Imperial State Crown.

Next, make your way to the **White Tower**, the original 11th century keep of the fortress, and the oldest Medieval part of the Tower of London. The keep was traditionally the strongest building providing accommodation for the king and his representatives as well as the country's armaments. When it was built it would have been the most menacing of buildings at around 30 m (98 ft) high, with its massive stone walls as much as 5 m (16 ft) thick in places. At that time it towered over the surrounding area and could be seen from far and wide and was as scary from the river as from land. Nowadays, in the shadow of and dwarfed by city skyscrapers it appears quite tame and it is a little difficult to imagine how threatening it must once have been.

During the reign of Henry III in the 13th century, this important Tower was whitewashed and subsequently became known as the 'White Tower'. As such, the iconic building has always been the nerve-centre of the Tower of London. It is especially famous today for its well-preserved Anglo-Norman church architecture in the Chapel of St John the Evangelist. It is one of the earliest Romanesque chapels in the country and you can still see the marvelous barrel-vaulted roof, rounded arches, and sturdy piers, so typical of the time when it was built in the late 11th/early 12th century.

It was here that Mary Tudor was betrothed by proxy to Philip of Spain in the 1550s and where Henry VII's wife, Elizabeth of York, was laid in state following her death in childbirth. With its bare walls and lack of decoration the chapel now looks quite plain but it is thought that it would originally have been brightly painted and further adorned by the beautiful stained glass windows added in Henry III's reign.

Over the years numerous changes were made to the White Tower and it was used for many different purposes, but for 500 years right up until the 19th century it was the main store for the nation's arsenal. As you walk around the White Tower today there are glass cabinets displaying magnificent examples of the royal armour of Tudor and Stuart Kings; Henry VIII, Charles I and James II, as well as gifts of armour given to the English sovereigns by foreign monarchs and leaders (a good example being the Armour of the Great Mogul presented to James I by the son of the Shogun Ieyasu in 1610). Two stunning suits of Henry VIII's armour dominate the display: one is his armour for man and horse made around 1520 when the king was both young and athletic, had a 91.5 cm (36 in) chest, and was very fit, the other is a much larger piece made about 20 years later when the king had put on a substantial amount of weight.

Armour was the way in which the European monarchs of the period went about one-upmanship. So excellent was the armour produced in the countries of northern Europe that Henry VIII felt compelled to set up his own workshop at Greenwich Palace in 1511 which he staffed with Italian, then Flemish and finally Flanders and German craftsmen. The 1515 'silvered and engraved'

armour made for Henry and his horse at
the Greenwich workshop is covered with
exquisite ornamentation, decorated with
the emblems of his and his wife's houses,
the Tudor rose and the pomegranate of the
Aragons, and the skirt is embellished with
the initials H and K. Henry may have worn
this armour at local tournaments or for the
1520 Field of the Cloth of Gold when he
joined with his French counterpart, King
Francis I for two weeks of flamboyant and
extravagant festivities. A perfect fit for
Henry's body it would have shown off his
athletic physique, his might, and would
have acted as a status symbol confirming
his affluence and rank.

Following Henry's death in 1547
although the royal Greenwich workshops
continued making armour into the next
century, neither Queen Mary I (1553–58)
nor Queen Elizabeth I (1558–1603) had
need of them so armour was purchased
by members of the court instead. Still
made to impress the items were beautifully
crafted and highly adorned and also very
expensive. To be wearing armour of this
calibre was making a statement – no
different to many rich and famous today
driving around in a Ferrari, sailing around

the Mediterranean in an enormous yacht or kitted out in cutting edge designer clothing.

Another major highlight of the White Tower and said to be the country's oldest tourist attraction is the **Line of Kings.** Dating back over 350 years it was an early piece of propaganda with the intention of promoting the king's right to rule. Consisting of a series of royal figures mounted on life-size carved wooden horses the Line of Kings included 'good' kings such as Edward III and Henry VIII, but omitted Edward II and Richard III who were considered to be 'bad'. Some of the carving was carried out in Grinling Gibbons woodcarving workshop and by other notable British woodcarvers. The always popular attraction appeared in London guidebooks from the mid 18th century. In later years the figures of Kings William III, George I and II were added and the Line of Kings was re-displayed periodically. Although in the 21st century we might consider the theme a little old-fashioned it is a charming collection that offers an insight into what appealed to visitors in times gone by.

In the minds of many the Tower of London has become synonymous with torture yet it was only during a short period in the 16th and 17th centuries that it was carried out to any great extent. Many people were imprisoned here but only a relatively small number actually underwent torture. To discover the instruments used in the turbulent times go to the **Torture at the Tower exhibition** beneath the Wakefield Tower (just by the group entrance gate) and imagine how anyone could defy their use. See the Scavenger's Daughter that compressed a person's body, the Rack, that stretched the victim resulting in dislocation of the limbs, and the Manacle, iron handcuffs which allowed the prisoner to be hung with his/her feet above the floor! Although only replicas of the actual instruments used they demonstrate only too well how prisoners would be made to suffer during the religious upheavals of the Tudor and early Stuart periods.

On leaving the exhibition look out for the **Tower Ravens** who lodge in front of the White Tower. They have been guardians of the Tower since the 1660s and are looked after by the Ravenmaster who ensures they are well cared for and are fed with raw meat twice a day. You will often see them roaming around the precincts but take care to keep your distance as they can bite if disturbed!

Now walk up the stairs ahead onto **Tower Green** where you will see the scaffold site, the place of execution of Queens Anne Boleyn and Katherine Howard and Lady Jane Grey. Only those of high-rank or nobility were killed here, rather than on Tower Hill outside the fortress precincts and it was considered a great privilege to be spared an execution away from the masses. In both locations a scaffold would be erected before the event and execution would be at the hands of the axe-man. Unusually, Anne Boleyn was an exception to this practice choosing to be beheaded by an expert French swordsman, brought over to London especially for the task.

Despite having a straightforward execution in 1554, it is said that Lady Jane Grey's ghost has appeared several times at the Tower. The last sighting occurred in 1957, four centuries after her death when two Guardsmen witnessed a white shape on the battlements.

Before leaving Tower Green you might be interested in seeing some prisoner graffiti written on the walls of nearby Beauchamp Tower. It was here that Lady Jane Grey's husband, Lord Guildford Dudley was held prisoner before his trial and subsequent execution, and a carving on the wall is believed to be of her name, 'Iane' (Jane).

By now you will probably have noticed the Yeoman Warders in their wonderful grand dark blue and red 'undress' uniforms (the ordinary duty uniforms and less elaborate than clothing worn on ceremonial occasions). They are in fact a detachment of the Yeoman of the Guard and have been the Royal Bodyguard for over 500 years. There are presently 37 Yeoman Warders at the Tower (including the Chief Yeoman Warder and Yeoman Gaoler), and all have served as Senior Non-Commissioned Officers in the armed forces with an honorable record for at least 22 years. They live on site with their families and so the Tower is their home! Full of wonderful anecdotes about the fortress and its inhabitants they are splendid storytellers. What better way to learn about Tower myths and stories than to join one of their regular tours (starting at the Byward Tower near the main entrance) that take place at half hourly intervals during the day. Most entertaining and full of grisly information, the tours last about 45 minutes concluding with a visit to the Chapel Royal of St Peter ad Vincula where the three executed queens are buried as well as Saints Thomas More and John Fisher.

The Yeoman Warders are more commonly known as **'Beefeaters'**, perhaps due to the fact that as members of the Royal Bodyguard they were allowed to eat as much beef as they wanted from the sovereign's table. Even though this practice no longer exists Yeoman Warders still carry out state duties: they attend the coronation of the sovereign, lying-in-state, and the annual Lord Mayor's Show. Every evening they participate in the Ceremony of the Keys, a ritual that has been taking place for over 700 years! Tickets for the ceremony can be obtained by application to the Tower of London but this is something you will need to do well in advance as it is a very popular event.

Before ending your tour you might want to spend some time in the **Medieval Palace** in the south perimeter wall close to Traitor's Gate. This gives you an idea how a Medieval king would have lived in the fortress and contains recreations of the furnishings of the period. When you leave the palace follow the **Wall Walk** which shows the enormous scale of the perimeter walls. It is an intriguing way to see the Tower and its precincts and get the feel of the breadth and extent of the fortress defences. The walks pass through seven large towers each of which is devoted to a different aspect of life in the Tower of London eg: Royal Beasts, the Duke of Wellington (Miltary Hero, former Constable of the Tower and Prime Minister), an exhibition of English royal crowns and an account of the 1381 Peasant's Revolt when the unruly mob managed to storm and breach the 'inpenetrable' fortress defences, beheading the Archbishop of Canterbury who was both a key politician as well as an important cleric.

From the walks there are excellent external views of the River Thames and Tower Bridge as well as the White Tower. As you walk along you might want to imagine how Tower prisoners, allowed to exercise on these walkways, would have felt seeing the strong defences and knowing how difficult, if not impossible, it would be to escape.

Fortunately, you are not imprisoned here and remain free to enjoy your visit. If you have timed it right you might manage to see costumed actors performing on the lawn outside the White Tower. Close by is the New Armouries Restaurant providing light and main meals or if you prefer to picnic snacks are available at the Raven's Kiosk close to the ravens' lodgings by the Wakefield Tower. Adjacent to the kiosk is the Raven shop selling all types of souvenirs and items relating to the Tower. The exit is close by and will lead you out on to Tower Wharf right by the river. From here you can take excellent photographs of Tower Bridge and the south

bank with its skyline of **City Hall** (the Mayor of London's administrative building), a wall of glass-fronted office blocks and **HMS Belfast**, the WWII battleship cruiser, moored alongside the river. Stroll eastwards along the Wharf, go under the bridge arch and walk into St Katharine Dock.

St Katharine Dock

Right next to the Tower, St Katharine Dock is a real treat with its colorful marina, boutique shops, cafes, bars and restaurants. This is the ideal place for relaxing and watching the world go by. To see it today it is sometimes difficult to visualize its early less commercial past.

Although the first dock appeared here almost 900 years ago, in 1147 Queen Matilda established a hospital and monastery on the site and a community settled into the neighbourhood. Over the years the population grew substantially but by the early 19th century the area had degenerated into a slum. Around this time the huge and rapid growth of the British Empire meant that London was in dire need of modern docks. In 1825 an Act of Parliament was passed giving the go-ahead for the development of St Katharine Dock; the existing hospital and church were demolished and the entire community (almost 11,000) evicted. It was an enormous project involving 2,500 workers moving the rubble and soil. The debris was subsequently placed in barges and taken up the Thames to be used in the foundations of Thomas Cubitt's housing developments for the wealthy in Pimlico and Belgravia to the west of London. The dock was in operation by 1828 and soon became renowned for its high-end luxury goods such as ivory, feathers, shells, marble, wine, tea and brandy.

St Katharine Dock was built by railway engineer, Thomas Telford, with two connected basins accessed through a lock to the River Thames, and boasted an unexpectedly long quay. Warehouses were constructed on the dockside with roadways immediately behind helping the loading process and also reducing the likelihood of theft.

Unfortunately, by the 1960s St Katharine, like its sister docks in the East End and across the river, was struggling badly. It had never completely recovered from the severe bomb damage of WWII and was also suffering from new practices implemented by the shipping industry in the post-war period. The introduction of shipping containers for cargo required much larger vessels and the existing docks were unable to accommodate them so new docks with deeper waters were built further east of London. Ultimately, St Katharine Dock was among the first of London's docklands to close down. Following a complete restoration starting in the early 1970s, a marina was built in the former basin area, warehouses were renovated and transformed for use as offices, loft apartments and housing as well as specialist shops and the dock was given a new lease of life. Bars, restaurants and cafes sprung up on the quayside and a Medieval Banquet opened in the Ivory House, one of the original buildings to survive the transformation from dock to marina and tourist attraction. In its heyday the elegant Ivory House had been a repository for the most exotic of goods including live turtles and exotic spices, and renowned throughout London for storing luxury goods from all four corners of the world.

Despite losing its original use the Ivory House remains a central feature of the marina today. It is very easy to while away time sitting in its shadow or in one of the many cafes or restaurants around the basin soaking up the atmosphere of boats and yachts and maybe thinking of times gone by. St Katharine Docksfrequently hosts boating events like the Clipper Round the World Yacht Race and Classic Boat Festival, which are hugely popular and bring many visitors to the marina and former dock.

Perhaps you might like to grab a bite to eat here, watch the boats enter and leave the marina or just enjoy the idyllic surroundings before visiting London's most iconic bridge.

TOWER BRIDGE AND THE DESIGN MUSEUM

First climb the stairs on to the bridge and walk south. Although it appears much older, Tower Bridge was erected only 120 years ago, designed by Horace Jones (known for his work at Leadenhall, Billingsgate and Smithfield Markets), and built in the Gothic style to complement the Tower of London. Recognized throughout the world as a major London landmark the bridge is a source of great enjoyment to many who regularly watch its two great bascules opening to allow shipping on the River Thames to pass through. A visit to the **Tower Bridge Exhibition** allows you to go right inside the bridge, find out about its construction and also visit the original steam-driven machinery of the bascules, a marvel of 19th century Victorian engineering. In 2015 a glass floor was added to the high-level walkway allowing you to look directly down on to the road bridge and see it in motion when it is opened up to accommodate river traffic. Details regarding bridge openings can be found on *www.towerbridge.org.uk*

In its heyday the bridge was raised about 5,000 times each year and the waters in front of the Tower of London were filled with all matter of sailing vessels; lighters, wherries, rowing boats. Indeed, so many were 'parked' here that you could pass from one side of the river to the other by jumping from boat to boat! This area, known as the Pool of London, has always been important to London and wharves and quays lined the river on both sides reflecting the industry of the area. Since the 1960s when the docks established themselves further down river in Tilbury, many of the old warehouses have been converted into residential accommodation, with excellent views of Tower Bridge, the Tower of London and the River Thames.

From the walkways if you look downstream (eastwards) you can see rising in the distance what appears to be a mini Manhattan. This is Canary Wharf, an area of Docklands which has been substantially altered and now houses many financial and banking organisations as well as newspapers. It is easily reached on the Docklands Light Railway (DLR) from Bank Underground Station,

Tower Gateway (DLR), as well as the Jubilee Line and has large shopping malls, restaurants, bars and even its own museum, the Museum of London in Docklands. More and more buildings are being added to the original 1980s development and it is becoming more like London's third city centre, after the City of London and the West End.

Alternative activity

If, after your busy morning you'd prefer just to have a leisurely stroll, I'd suggest that you walk across Tower Bridge, descend the stairs at the far end down to the **Thames Riverside Walk**. For a feel of how the area would have looked when the docks were busy and prosperous turn left (eastwards) walking through Shad Thames and see the over-hanging walkways that connected the warehouses to the quayside. Cut through left on to the river path from where you will have really good views of Tower Bridge. Along this stretch you will come across many restaurants and London's Design Museum, due to move to west London in 2016, which is well worth a visit, time permitting.

The Design Museum

Located in what was originally a banana warehouse, the Design Museum was founded by Sir Terence Conran in 1989, and transformed into its current International Modernist style building. The permanent collection concentrates on product design both in the home and at the office.

Throughout the year a number of temporary exhibitions are held covering fashion, furniture, architecture, graphics, product and digital design and the museum also offers a full programme of events, talks, and family activities. The Blueprint Café, with wonderful views of the Thames and Tower Bridge is found on the first floor, and there is a small café and shop downstairs.

Now, re-trace your steps and go west alongside the river, passing by City Hall, the Headquarters of London's elected mayor and administration, and an area of glass-fronted office buildings. Standing here you are well placed to take photographs of Tower Bridge, sites on the north bank, the Tower of London and the City of London.

Nearby, the battleship cruiser, HMS Belfast, part of the Imperial War Museum, is open daily (admission charge). This is an ideal stop if you are travelling with children giving them the chance to investigate the ship's nine decks and to discover what life was like on board for the crew during the Belfast's working life between 1939 and 1963.

Just a little further along the pathway you reach Hay's Galleria, a thriving dock in the 19th century when it accommodated great ocean going vessels. So busy was the area at that time that it earned the nickname 'London's Larder' receiving regular deliveries of tea from the Far East, dairy produce, lamb, coffee and cocoa. However, with the changes in London's docklands in the late 20th century the dock was redeveloped and has become a complex full of shops, stalls, cafes and restaurants – a great spot to chill out and an insight into times gone by.

TOWER OF LONDON: PAST AND PRESENT

TOWER PAST

Daring Escapes!

Despite the height and size of its walls, prisoners have managed to escape from the Tower on several occasions and with apparent ease!

The first to do so was Ranulf Flambard, Bishop of Durham, in 1100. Incarcerated during Henry I's reign, accused of extortion, he managed to dupe his guards by getting them into a heavy drunken stupor and then taking advantage of their state to use a smuggled rope and climb out of the window of his room. Even though the rope was a little short and didn't reach the ground, he managed to jump down successfully and was met by friends who then spirited him away (allegedly on a waiting horse).

Almost 500 years later, in the late 16th century, another bold escape was made by Father John Gerard. A Jesuit priest, he was being held in the Salt Tower and whilst there spent much of his day writing letters to people. This activity appeared innocent enough and no one thought to question what he wrote or to whom he was writing. He was in fact, creating a group of followers writing to them in invisible orange juice and passing on secret information. He corresponded in this manner with a fellow Catholic prisoner, John Arden, imprisoned in the nearby Cradle Tower. Having persuaded a guard to let them get together to celebrate Mass, the two hatched an escape plan which they later put into effect. Remarkably, they managed to climb down the Cradle Tower, swing across the moat to a waiting boat and retain their freedom!

The most recent and perhaps intrepid escape, was made in the 18th century by William Maxwell, Lord Nithsdale. Unlike the two earlier prisoners, Nithsdale was detained within the Lieutenant's Lodgings on Tower Green where he was awaiting execution. The night before the event was due to take place he was visited by his wife and her two friends who distracted the guards with their crying and wailing whilst Nithsdale dressed himself in women's clothing, and then brazenly walked out with the group at the end of their visit. Amazingly, the deception worked and his absence was not immediately discovered. Nithsdale left England at once and made his way to Rome masquerading as a servant to a Venetian ambassador, and was later joined by his wife.

Crown Jewel Heist – 1671

This was a most audacious plot carried out by an Anglo-Irish officer, Colonel Thomas Blood, to steal the Crown Jewels displayed in the Tower of London. These were a very valuable new set of jewels that had been created for King Charles II's Coronation ceremony in 1661, the original ones having been destroyed during the Cromwellian Commonwealth years (1649–60).

After the Coronation the jewels were kept within the Martin Tower on the inner wall of the Tower and a Keeper appointed to look after them. By paying a small viewing fee the famous collection could be seen by members of the public. Blood, dressed as a clergyman and accompanied by his so-called wife, came to view the Crown Jewels and managed to ingratiate himself with the elderly custodian, Talbot Edwardes and his wife, making arrangements to return to see them with their 'nephew' who would be a very good match for the couple's daughter. When he returned Blood, together with his conspirators overcame Edwardes, tying him up and when the custodian resisted they struck and stabbed him. The group then ran off with the crown, an orb and sceptre, but due to a series of events, their escape was foiled and the crown jewels re-captured.

The strangest part of the story is however its ending! Blood, despite having been caught stealing the most precious royal possessions, was given a full pardon by King Charles II and even awarded a pension of £500. No one knows how he managed to escape execution for his deeds, but many theories exist! It is said that perhaps the king himself had set up the heist as he was in dire need of cash, he may have just liked the roguish Blood or admired his audacity, so felt inclined to pardon him. Or maybe Blood was on the king's payroll working as a spy? It is certainly a mystery and one to this day that continues to provide speculation.

Tower Present

Throughout the summer and autumn of 2014 the Tower moat took on an entirely new look and was visited by over five million people. They came to see the **Blood Swept Lands and Seas of Red** ceramic poppy installation, the work of Paul Cummins (ceramic artist) and Tom Piper (theater designer), remembering the 888,246 from the UK and Commonwealth who lost their lives in military combat during WWI.

Cummins' idea of filling the moat with hand-made poppies was truly inspirational and the installation, which could be seen surrounding the entire tower, became a wonderful fitting tribute to those who had died in the conflict. Each poppy (costing £25) was individually crafted and came with its own certificate, a commemorative booklet in a presentation box, and a stem and fixing. Sales of the ceramic flowers were reported to have raised over £10 million and this was subsequently shared between six service charities offering support and aid to war veterans and their families.

It took four months to 'plant' the poppy field and the work was carried out by a team of 17,000 volunteers; some had lost family in conflicts, others had serving relatives overseas, whilst many just wanted to be involved in the creation of what they considered to be such a significant enterprise.

During the 'planting' the Last Post was played each night at sunset to remember those who were killed in the 1914–1918 War. The final poppy was planted on 11 November, Armistice Day, after which the poppies were distributed to their buyers. It was agreed that only two sections of the installation, the Wave (located by the causeway) and cascading Weeping Window sculptures should be retained. On tour around the UK until 2018 these sculptures will later be on permanent display at the Imperial War Museum in London and Manchester.

SECTION TWO

RIVER CRUISE TO GREENWICH

The River Thames, today used mainly by leisure craft, is the perfect route to take for a trip to Greenwich. Tickets can be booked at the river piers or on-line through *www.thamesriverservices.co.uk* usually with a discount for on-line bookings, *www.Thamesclippers.com* (a faster commuter service), or with *www.citycruises.com*. All offer a selection of tickets and provide details about the piers used and timings of their services on their websites, giving you excellent choice. Some boats have an open-air deck as well as an interior saloon and you'll be sure to have good views of London sights and skyline wherever you sit.

It is a real joy to travel down from Westminster to Greenwich passing the many iconic landmarks and buildings; see the London Eye by Westminster Bridge, Cleopatra's Needle, Somerset House, The Royal Festival Hall and South Bank complex, the National Theater, Tate Modern, the Globe Theater, Tower of London, and pass under Tower Bridge sailing on to Canary Wharf and then finally on to the UNESCO World Heritage Site of Greenwich. Approaching the town from the river affords you the most splendid panorama, and shows off the old Royal Naval College (now the University of Greenwich and Trinity School of Music) on the riverside with its backdrop of Greenwich Park and the Royal Observatory at its very best.

The journey times are governed by the tides as well as river traffic but generally the trip lasts about an hour from Westminster, slightly longer for the return journey and some, but not all of the boats provide commentary as you travel along the river.

Alternatively, take a Jubilee Line underground train from central London to

Canary Wharf, and then change on to the Docklands Light Railway (DLR) in the direction of Lewisham alighting at Cutty Sark for Maritime Greenwich. You can reach the same station directly on the DLR from Bank Underground Station.

MARITIME GREENWICH: THE CUTTY SARK AND OLD ROYAL NAVAL COLLEGE

Although only a mere four miles from Tower Bridge the town has a real identity of its own and summer or winter, it promises the visitor a good time. 'Maritime Greenwich' describes a cluster of its famous buildings: The Old Royal Naval College with its Painted Hall and Chapel, Queen's House, the National Maritime Museum and the Royal Observatory, which since 1997 have been jointly designated as a UNESCO World Heritage Site.

Before exploring these impressive buildings you might want to step aboard the fastest and last surviving tea clipper of its day, the **Cutty Sark**, found close to the waterfront. You will easily locate the ship near to the river recognizable by her rigging and masts. An unusual name, 'Cutty Sark' meaning short shirt, the title is taken from the poem 'Tam O'Shanter', by Scottish poet, Robert Burns. In the poem he nicknamed the witch, Nannie Dee, Cutty Sark.

The clipper is open for viewing daily from 10am-5pm, last entry 4pm, and is unlikely to disappoint you. Since major restoration work between 2006–2012 it can now be seen from both above deck and below its hull in an enclosed exhibition space within the dry dock; this totally new experience allows you to admire the very advanced technology that was used to make the ship so fast and enable it to cross thousands of miles of ocean.

The vessel was built on Clydeside, Scotland, and had her maiden voyage in 1869. Initially put to use in the China tea trade, she later carried coal between China and Australia, and wool from Australia to London and New York. She sailed to all the world's major ports as a cargo ship until 1922 when she was saved for the nation by Captain Wilfred Dowmen and was brought to Greenwich in 1954 where she has been berthed ever since. On board there is much to see and learn about life at sea and to discover about Cutty Sark's gripping history. There is a wonderful collection of figureheads on show as well as information about the vessel, its measurements, owners, and crew.

The town of Greenwich has in fact always had a rich sea-faring history and royal heritage. From the early 15th century when Humphrey, Duke of Gloucester built his riverside palace, Bellacourt, in Greenwich, royalty resided here. Towards the end of the 1400s the first Tudor monarch, King Henry VII developed his palace, which then became known as the Palace of Placentia. His son, Henry VIII, was born here and spent a carefree youth jousting and hunting in the palace grounds and parklands. It became a favourite too of subsequent Tudor and early Stuart monarchs, though in time it became neglected and was ultimately demolished to make way for the Old Royal Naval College. This building was designed and built between 1696–1712 by Sir Christopher Wren (also responsible for St Paul's Cathedral and many of the re-built City churches after the Great Fire of London in 1666). The stunning symmetry and architecture of this building with its twin domed towers still remains, and although no longer used for its original purpose as a Royal Hospital for Seamen, it is now home to the University of Greenwich, the Trinity College of Music and Dance and the Trinity Laban Conservatoire.

The Greenwich Foundation manages the site and opens two of its architectural treasures to the public, namely the Painted Hall and Chapel. These two buildings nowadays are decorated in entirely different styles, yet both have to be seen! **The Painted Hall** owes its appearance to the artist James Thornhill (who painted the Dome of St Paul's Cathedral) and contains brilliant flamboyant Baroque paintings on the walls and ceilings. The Hall itself was used on a daily basis by both seamen and their officers, and when Admiral Nelson died his body laid in state here in January 1806 before his funeral ceremony at St Paul's Cathedral.

The Chapel, situated opposite the Painted Hall is a complete contrast; light and airy it seems far less fussy and opulent but is still very grand and is wonderfully decorated in the neo-Grecian style.

NATIONAL MARITIME MUSEUM, GREENWICH AND PANORAMIC VIEWS!

Across the road from the chapel you can visit the **National Maritime Museum**, part of the World Heritage site, and full of galleries which detail Britain's maritime heritage. The gallery's collection is vast containing memorabilia associated with Admiral Nelson (including his uniform worn at the Battle of Trafalgar where he met his death), ship models and plans, maritime art, and galleries devoted to British maritime trade with Africa, Slavery, Trade and Empire. Admission is free to all permanent galleries but charges are made for temporary exhibitions.

Right next to the main body of the museum is the **Queen's House**, which is where the museum's fine art collection is on display. The 17th century house is itself an architectural gem, and the first in its style to be built in the country. Designed by Inigo Jones for James I's wife, Anne of Denmark, it contains a remarkable double-height galleried Hall (Jones's inspiration having come from the Italian Renaissance buildings he had encountered during his travels in Italy).

Sadly, Anne of Denmark died before the building was completed and it was her daughter-in-law, Henrietta Maria, wife of Charles I, who eventually lived in the beautiful building.

Stretching behind the house is London's oldest Royal Park, **Greenwich Park**, enclosed by King Henry VIII some 500 years ago for hunting deer. Probably best known throughout the world for being the starting place of the annual televised London Marathon, and also as the venue of the 2012 London Olympic Games equestrian trials and events, including showjumping and dressage.

The grounds are very popular; local residents and visitors enjoy its wide, open spaces, boating pond, gardens and deer park. Walk through the park and up

the hill to reach the Royal Observatory on its peak. It is a steep climb so be warned!

At the summit take time out and stop by the statue of General Wolfe and wonder at the panorama in front of you. This is undoubtedly the most spectacular, breathtaking view. Directly below at the base of the hill you see the architectural beauty of the Queen's House and Old Royal Naval College. Further in the distance your eyes are drawn to the towers of Canary Wharf on the Isle of Dogs. Over to the right you catch sight of the 2012 Olympic Stadium and on a clear day looking to the left you might well catch a glimpse of the heights of Hampstead in North London.

ROYAL OBSERVATORY

Now make your way to **Flamsteed House**, the original **Royal Observatory** building designed by Sir Christopher Wren for the Astronomer Royal, Sir John Flamsteed, in 1675. Note that unlike the Maritime Museum a charge is made for entry to Flamsteed House with its Time Galleries and the Meridian Courtyard.

The Meridian Line, set outside in the Courtyard represents the Prime Meridian of the World – Longitude 0. It not only separates the earth's eastern and western hemispheres but every place throughout the globe is measured by its length east or west from this line. Standing in the courtyard, home of Greenwich Mean Time, is the only place where you can stand astride the two hemispheres simultaneously.

Before entering Flamsteed House look up at the vivid red time ball on the top of the house. At a time before people owned their own watches or clocks, this was one of the first public time signals, allowing maritime vessels on the Thames and Londoners to know the time. Since 1833 the ball rises daily up to its mast at 12.55 and five minutes later it falls, signifying it is 1pm.

As Flamsteed House was built as both a home and workplace for Astronomers

Royal you enter through its domestic apartments before arriving in the Time Galleries where John Harrison's 18th century timekeepers H1–H4 are displayed. These are the machines that ultimately found the solution to keeping precise time at sea which was so sorely needed in the 1700s. Harrison's design was the real breakthrough and revolutionised navigation for traders and explorers of the period, but he had to wait many years until late in the 18th century before he was awarded the £20,000 Longitude prize for his invention.

There is much detailed information about the Royal Observatory and its collections on the museums website, *www.rmg.co.uk* which may help you to plan your visit. The website also provides the schedule of the shows at London's planetarium which is based alongside the Royal Observatory.

Now, leave the park and return to the waterfront area. If you are visiting

between Thursday and Sunday you will be able to explore **Greenwich Market** which specializes in arts and crafts. Situated in a lovely covered yard it boasts a great variety of stalls selling anything from clothing and jewellery to antique silverware and food too! There are pubs, bars and cafes at every turn and lots of small boutiques to browse in.

If you still have enough energy other nearby attractions in the town are **St Alfege Church**, **the Fan Museum** and the **Trafalgar Tavern** which in Victorian Britain served its renowned 'whitebait suppers' and was much frequented by politicians and literary giants such as Dickens and Thackeray.

At the end of your visit you might want to return to central London by boat in which case you should make your way to Greenwich Pier. Alternatively, you can take the DLR towards Tower Gateway or Bank Underground Station and link up with the underground from there.

Sunset panorama over the Thames

If you decide to take the river route, a couple of suggestions to round off your day: Either alight at London Bridge City Pier and make your way to London's tallest building**, the Shard**, (located next to London Bridge station) or continue to London Eye Pier to visit the **London Eye**. If you opt for the former, you will pay an entry charge (£5.00 cheaper if booked on-line 24 hours in advance) to enter the View From The Shard viewing gallery on the 69th floor. From here you will be rewarded with wonderful 360° views of London and on a clear day you might see up to forty miles from central London. You'll find touchscreen telescopes that allow you to view the details of London in close up and show you how places look at different times of the day. They also provide information about 200 major London sights. A further open-air viewing platform can be reached on Level 72 and here you can look right up to the very top of the building, an awe-inspiring, if perhaps, a little scary, experience!

Also within the Shard you'll find a mixture of restaurants and bars offering breakfast, lunch, afternoon tea, fine dining, cocktails and late night drinks – the ideal place to come for food and splendid views. Don't worry if you are afraid of external glass- sided elevators as the lifts within the building are internal and very fast, transporting you to the Viewing Gallery in about sixty seconds.

Alternatively, you could get off the boat outside the London Eye for a leisurely 'flight' on the wheel. The Eye has 32 pods, each one carrying 25 people, and moves so slowly that it almost comes as a surprise when you reach the top. As with the Shard you should be able to see a fair distance if the weather is clear, and it is certainly fun trying to identify well-known buildings and landmarks.

The London Eye has become so very established on the south bank that it now looks as though it has always been there. Literally millions have visited it since it opened in London for the Millennium with architects, husband and wife team, David Marks and Julia Barfield winning many awards for its design. Engineers from across Europe worked on the project and the wheel was constructed in stages with segments that had been floated down the Thames lifted into position to complete the structure.

Tickets can be purchased on arrival at the attraction but it is cheaper to book on-line at *www.londoneye.com*

You will find eating places close by as well as two popular attractions: The London Dungeon (*www.thedungeons.com/london*) and SEA LIFE London Aquarium (*www2.visitsealife.com/London*), which are of great appeal to families. The closest Underground Station is Waterloo (*Northern, Jubilee and Bakerloo lines*) or a short walk across Westminster Bridge brings you to Westminster Underground Station where you can pick up more of the tube network (*Circle, District and Jubilee lines*).

PICTURE CAPTIONS

1 - Tower of London

2 - Beefeater

3 - White Tower, Tower of London

4 - St Katharine Dock

5 - Tower Bridge

6 - Old Royal Naval College, Greenwich

7 - Cutty Sark, Greenwich

8 - Greenwich Park

9 - Prime Meridian, Greenwich

10 - London Eye

DAY 4

RIVERSIDE LONDON

SECTION ONE

ARTS AND THEATER

SOMERSET HOUSE – STRAND

Visit Somerset House at any time of the year and you are sure to find something to appeal. It is hard to believe that not so long ago, when the Inland Revenue had offices on site, the cobbled stone courtyard was used as a car park, but following a massive refurbishment in 2000 this all changed.

Today the courtyard (Edmond J Safra Fountain Court) is used for all manner of activities and arts events. In summer, when the 55 fountains are turned on, it

becomes a major venue for children and their families, and every August over a two week period the Film 4 Summer Screen takes place here nightly when classic and contemporary films are screened under the stars! Other events such as installations, art exhibitions and music concerts are also staged here. For two months during the winter the courtyard is home to an ice-skating rink and is busy day and night with visitors and locals alike whizzing around on the ice. This was the first of London's rinks and is still a firm favourite set in such a wonderful location.

There are a number of galleries situated in the blocks surrounding the main courtyard. **The Courtauld Gallery** (*www.courtauld.ac.uk*) beside the main entrance is a small though most impressive art gallery, famous in particular for its Impressionist and Post-Impressionist art collection. Here you will find Van Gogh's 'Self-Portrait with Bandaged Ear', Paul Cezanne's 'The Card Players', as well as equally well-known works of artists such as Degas, Manet, Gaugain, Monet and Renoir. The collection also contains 20th century art (both British and European) and a Renaissance collection. Temporary exhibitions are held in the **Terrace and Courtyard Rooms** as well as in the **East and West Wing Galleries.**

The Embankment Galleries, located in the basement of Somerset House by the riverside entrance, are used for temporary, specialist exhibitions, and generally concentrate on themes such as architecture, photography and contemporary fashion. 'Valentino: Master of Couture', and 'Isabella Blow: Fashion Galore!' have been two much acclaimed exhibitions in recent times.

History of Somerset House

The building standing here today is not the first on the site. In the 1500s the Duke of Somerset had built himself a very fine town house on this spot, which in later years was used as a residence by royalty. Queen Elizabeth I, before ascending the throne, lived at the house and it was from here that she rode out to welcome her sister Mary Tudor, to London as Queen. After her death, throughout the next century, the Catholic wives of three Stuart kings, Anne of Denmark (James I), Henrietta-Maria (Charles I) and Catherine of Braganza (Charles II), all resided here. Spectacular masques organized by Ben Jonson and Inigo Jones took place in the house whilst Anne of Denmark resided here.

Ultimately, the building was demolished in the middle of the 18th century to make way for the first purpose-built office block in the capital! Built in the then fashionable Palladian style this was initially used by a group of royal societies as well as the Navy and Stamp (Tax) office, and a little later by the offices of the Register of Births, Deaths and Marriages. None of these organisations remain on the site today although a variety of cultural and artistic companies are now based here reflecting the use of Somerset House as a major arts and cultural centre.

Film makers have naturally recognized the beauty of the setting and incorporated both the building and courtyard in a number of films, *Shanghai Nights* (2003) with Jackie Chan and Owen Wilson, *Last Chance Harvey* with Dustin Hoffman and Emma Thompson (2006), *Sherlock Holmes* with Jude Law and Robert Downey Jr. (2009) as well as TV dramas and fashion shoots.

As you would expect there are several eating places here as well as a lovely riverside terrace bar (open during the spring and summertime) overlooking the Thames and with outstanding views both up and downstream.

At the end of your visit take the Embankment Galleries exit. Cross the Victoria Embankment to walk alongside the river and turn left walking towards the City of London. You will see across the water another of London's major cultural centres, the National Theater complex. Easily recognizable owing to its grey concrete Brutalist style, this centre houses three theaters as well as other temporary performance spaces. Despite its somewhat gloomy exterior it is a very welcoming and comfortable centre buzzing with life and has a well-deserved reputation for putting on reasonably priced and consistently good plays ranging from contemporary through to Shakespearean to ancient Greek tragedy.

When you reach Blackfriars Bridge turn right to walk across it to the south bank. Your view east is somewhat obstructed by the adjacent railway bridge at Blackfriars, however you have some excellent views west (to your right) and should be able to catch sight of the Oxo Tower and London Eye on the south side of the river, and the gardens of the Inns of Court, the home of London's lawyers, on the north side.

Cross the bridge and just before the end walk down a short flight of stairs on to the river path, where, facing the river you turn right. After passing Blackfriars Station entrance and the Founders Arms pub on the riverfront you will see a large red-brick building with a lofty tower looming up on the right. This is Tate Modern.

TATE MODERN

It is easy to understand why Tate Modern is one of London's most popular attractions. Its sheer scale, owing to its original construction as a power station, as well as the extent of its international modern art collection have enticed literally millions through its doors since it first opened in 2000.

Herzog and de Meuron, the Swiss architects, transformed the power station's entrance Turbine Hall which had previously housed the enormous generators into a cavernous space suitable for large-scale installations. Since the outset there have been regular sponsored installations on display here: Louise Bourgeois's giant steel spider, the very first of the Unilever Series, was highly praised. More recently, Carsten Holler's fun helter-skelter rides, Ai Weiwei's hand-crafted ceramic sunflower seeds, and Olafur Eliasson's, the Weather Project which involved visitors lying down on the Turbine Hall floor and basking in fake sunshine, have been similarly acclaimed. The Gallery has become so popular that it is in the midst of an ambitious expansion project which will result in a new eleven floor landmark structure built to the south of the existing gallery. The extension is due to open in June 2016 and will allow Tate Modern to double its present exhibition space and ensure greater room to display performance and installation art.

At present Tate Modern's permanent collection is arranged both chronologically and by theme in spaces entitled Energy and Process, Making Traces, Poetry and Dream and Structure and Clarity. It includes works of pop artists, cubists, surrealists and most 'isms' of 20th century and contemporary art. Displayed in four main areas the Gallery frequently rotates what it exhibits to allow visitors to see as much of the collection as possible but you are likely to see the works of leading international artists such as Lichtenstein, Warhol, Braque, Picasso, Rothko, Mondrian, Matisse, Joseph Beuys, Rebecca Horn, Jackson Pollock and Kandinsky as well as a good selection of modern British art including works by Lucien Freud and David Hockney as well as YBA's (Young British Artists), like Damien Hirst and Tracey Emin.

The gallery is open daily between 10am and 6pm with extended opening every Friday and Saturday until 10pm. This is a lovely time to visit as the restaurant located on Level 6 (which has superb views of both St Paul's Cathedral and the Millennium Bridge) also stays open and you can experience an evening of culture whilst enjoying excellent food in beautiful surroundings.

In addition to the restaurant there is a large Riverside café on Level 1 and an Espresso Bar on Level 3 serving light snacks and refreshments. The bookshop just beside the Turbine Hall is so well stocked with the most comprehensive selection of art books that once inside it can be truly difficult to drag yourself away.

Families visiting the gallery are well catered for too with family multi-media guides and a daily kids activity section on the Level 2 concourse. Throughout the gallery there are many interactive exhibits and children will enjoy the digital drawing bar on Level 3, where they are free to demonstrate their creativity.

Tate Modern is in fact, one of four Tate art galleries in the UK today. Two are based outside London, in Liverpool in the north and St Ives in Cornwall, whilst Tate Britain is a short distance away along the Thames in Pimlico, close to Lambeth Bridge. The first Tate Gallery was set up in 1897 by the sugar magnate, Henry Tate (inventor of the sugar cube and subsequently a very wealthy man), who collected British and contemporary art. The gallery was originally known as **National Gallery of British Art (Millbank)** but soon became known as the **Tate**. Towards the end of the twentieth century, as the holder of the British art collection from the 16ᵗʰ century as well as international modern and contemporary art the Tate found that it was running out of space hence the decision to split the collection and to open a new museum that would exhibit Modern Art since 1900. At this point the gallery in Pimlico became **Tate Britain** (exhibiting British Art to the present day) and the new gallery, was named Tate Modern.

If you are interested in seeing more of the Tate collection at Tate Britain take the Tate to Tate boat, operated by Thames Clippers, from the pier outside the gallery. The boat runs every 40 minutes whilst the gallery is open. It is a short journey upstream to Tate Britain, which is also free and opens daily.

Shakespeare's Globe Theater

Practically right next door to Tate Modern, just past the Millennium Bridge as you walk eastwards along the river path is the reconstruction of Shakespeare's Globe Theater. Although a remarkably close reproduction of the original 16ᵗʰ century playhouse it has only been in situ since 1995. Built, using the techniques and materials of the Elizabethan age, with green oak and wooden pegs to fix the timbers together, the theater was spearheaded by the US actor and film director, Sam Wanamaker. He campaigned for twenty-five years to get the project off the ground and to see a theater devoted to William Shakespeare in London, the city where the playwright/actor had performed and lived for most of his working life. It was due to his tireless efforts that the Globe Theater was built in this area, Bankside, which had been the home of London's entertainment in Elizabethan and Jacobean times, four hundred years ago. Admittedly, it has moved its location slightly, but the theater is an excellent copy of the Tudor theater with its galleried wooden covered seating and its central yard open to the skies. The present theater accommodates about 1500 people, a third of whom will stand in the yard right by the action and beside the performers. In Shakespeare's day the spectators who stood in the yard were called groundlings and were renowned for their often noisy, boisterous and bad behavior. Elizabethan theaters would often pack in their audiences into the auditorium with up to 3000 being a common occurrence.

Tickets, then as now, cost far less for groundlings than for those sitting up above on the covered seats, but don't be fooled into thinking that you will be much more comfortable. The wooden benches are very hard and it may be advisable to hire a cushion to sit on before the performance begins!

Due to its open roof the season runs only in the summer months starting on Shakespeare's birthday, 23rd April and lasting until October. The major part of the repertoire are Shakespeare's plays, though works of his contemporaries are put on, as well as new plays written especially for the theater. As you would expect the acting is invariably of the highest quality and standard and it can be difficult to book seats.

During the off-peak months (and mornings during the summer), guided tours of the theater run every thirty minutes. In addition, there is a most informative basement exhibition which gives an excellent account of the life and times of the playwright, as well as detailing how Sam Wanamaker established the Shakespeare's Globe Trust (SGT), showing how the building developed and was eventually constructed. It may be of interest to know that special permission had to be sought for the Globe's thatched roof before it could be built! Since the Great Fire of London in 1666 when 80% of London's houses and buildings were destroyed there has been a law forbidding such roofing in the capital. Fortunately consent to build the roof was granted thus allowing us to experience Shakespearean drama in very similar surroundings to the original 16th century performances.

Just behind Shakespeare's Globe is a recent addition: **the Sam Wanamaker Playhouse**. A small intimate space it is a typical indoor oak Jacobean theater with two horse-shoed galleries and benches in a pit. With seating for 340 the theater is almost entirely lit by candle-light, and ideal for winter productions. Completed at a cost of £7.5 million, its construction is based on 17th century plans for an indoor theater similar to the format of the Blackfriars Theater. The shell of the Playhouse was erected when Shakespeare's Globe theater was being constructed in the 1990s and initially used for rehearsals and educational workshops. The new theater opened in 2014 and is already the most popular venue. Although it remains open throughout the year it becomes the location for readings and concerts during the summer when the Globe's productions are performed. If you would like to attend a performance at either theater check the website, *www.shakespearesglobe.com* before your trip as seats are like gold-dust and get sold out fast.

To round off your visit to the complex you may want to sample the cuisine of the riverside restaurant and bar, The Swan, located on the first floor. Right beside the Thames it has magnificent river views and is an excellent spot to watch the throngs of people walking by.

Finally, to end your day, re-trace your steps along the river path towards Tate Modern and turn left up the ramp. You will be walking over the Millennium Bridge, the only pedestrian bridge to have been built across the river in central London for over 100 years! Opened to see in the new Millennium it was initially found to be unstable, giving rise to its nickname, 'The Wobbly Bridge'. The problem was quickly resolved and the bridge soon became a great favourite with Londoners and visitors alike. Linking the north and south banks of the Thames it is most convenient for locals who work in the City of London and live across the river. For visitors, it gives easy access from the entertainments and activities of the South Bank over to the historic 'Square Mile' of London.

Views from the bridge are simply stunning: look upstream and you see Westminster, Tate Modern and Shakespeare's Globe Theater, whilst downstream is Tower Bridge, the City of London, Canary Wharf and The Shard.

LONDON'S ANNUAL FESTIVALS AND EVENTS

Whatever time of the year you visit London you will be sure to find some festival or event in progress. Whilst some are traditional, like Trooping the Color and The Lord Mayor's Show, others are seasonal as Winter Wonderland in Hyde Park, or the Notting Hill Carnival held each August. The following list includes a selection of what is available on every theme from sport to music, the arts, architecture and pageantry and gives brief details about their location, timing and information about what to expect.

Remember! All these events attract great throngs of people so take good care of your possessions especially when in crowded places.

New Year's Day Parade - January

If you are in London at the New Year this is definitely the event to make for, ushering in the New Year with great festivity. Taking place between midday and 3.30pm, the Parade normally starts at Piccadilly near the Ritz Hotel and finishes at Parliament Square. Since it began in 1987 the event has become ever more popular and now attracts about 500,000 people spread out along the route. With over 8000 participants, it is a real spectacle and great fun for families. London boroughs are represented on imaginative, brightly colored floats, and marching bands from US universities and high schools together with their cheer leaders keep spectators entertained.

Oxford and Cambridge Boat Race - March/April

With the exception of war-time the race has been held annually since 1856, with Oxford donning dark blue colors and Cambridge wearing pale blue.

The race takes place at the end of March/early April over a 4.2 mile course on the river Thames, starting at Mortlake and ending at Putney, in west London. Thousands watch the rowing 8's encouraging them from the banks of the river, and the event is also televised. Currently (2015), Cambridge have won 81 times, and Oxford 79 and there has been one dead heat. It is the tradition for the loser to challenge the winner to a rematch in the following year.

The London Marathon - April

The London Marathon (currently sponsored by Virgin Money) is a phenomenal money-spinner having raised over £450 million for charity since it was first run in 1981. It is one of 6 major international marathons that is run over a distance of 26 miles and 385 yards and has attracted a greater number of participants and spectators each year.

Over three quarters of the participants use the race to raise money for good causes and it is not uncommon to see people dressed up as cartoon characters, or in fancy dress, loved by the crowds who cheer them on. Most of the course is run on flat ground around the Thames, beginning near Blackheath in south-east London and meandering along north and south banks of the Thames until the final stretch between Tower Hill and The Mall by St James's Park.

Little Venice Canalway Cavalcade - May

The Cavalcade is a splendid 3 day celebration that takes place annually on the May Bank Holiday weekend. To discover more about the event refer to the panel, Open Spaces, Waterways and Markets.

Trooping the Color - June

This is a military ceremony carried out by the Queen's personal troops, the Household Division (Foot Guards and the Household Cavalry) on Horseguards Parade. Celebrating the sovereign's official birthday the soldiers present their 'colors' (flag) to the Queen, who takes the Royal Salute and inspects her troops from her royal carriage. It is a lively event with massed bands performing a musical 'troop'. The ceremony itself dates from the 17th century when the colors of a regiment were used as a rallying point in battle and it was necessary for each soldier to recognize them.

The route of the procession is from Buckingham Palace via the Mall to Horseguards Parade and when the pageantry has ended the Queen with her family gather on the balcony at Buckingham Palace to watch a fly past by the RAF.

Tickets to the event are available by ballot in January/February each year but even without a ticket you may still be able to catch a glimpse of the troops and horses by standing on The Mall or from within St James's Park

Wimbledon Tennis - End June/July

Wimbledon, in south-west London, is home to the annual international tennis tournament involving star players from throughout the world. Held over a 2 week period it is one of London's major summer season events, and there is always great competition for tickets which may be obtained via a ballot (held in the autumn). Alternatively, you can queue on the day for tickets to Centre Court and Courts 1 and 2.

BBC Promenade Concerts - July–September

Held in the splendid Royal Albert Hall in Kensington, the 'Proms' take place over a two month period each year and culminate in the famous 'Last Night of the Proms'. It is the world's largest classical music festival which has enthralled its audiences for over 120 years. Look on the BBC website, *www.bbc.co.uk* to find out more about what is on offer and how to purchase tickets.

Notting Hill Carnival - August

This is a wonderfully noisy and lively carnival that takes place on the last weekend in August each year. With blaring Caribbean music, dancing, food and magnificent floats the area is simply teeming with people and it is one of

London's most exciting, boisterous, colorful and happy festivals.

London Open House Weekend - Mid Sept

This is the one and only weekend when many buildings, generally off limits to the public, open their doors without charge. Some are government departments, others civic halls, museums, gentlemen's clubs, university premises, tower blocks and even iconic city skyscrapers. It is the capital's annual festival of architecture and design and a fantastic opportunity to see some amazing interiors and views or gain access to some of the city's secret hidden treasures.

Lord Mayor's Show - November

To celebrate the start of the new Lord Mayor's year of office a spectacular show is put on in the City of London on the 2nd Saturday in November. Reflecting over 800 years of history and tradition a three mile procession takes place in the very heart of the City on a route that takes in Mansion House, St Paul's Cathedral, the Royal Courts of Justice and the Victoria Embankment by the side

of the Thames. Starting in the morning with a River Pageant, and followed by a procession with over 7000 participants and 150 floats that represent youth associations, foreign businesses, the livery companies and charities, the show offers something for everyone. A particular highlight of the day is seeing the new Lord Mayor go by in his very grand and elaborate coach, pulled by a team of six shire horses.

The Cenotaph, Remembrance Sunday - November

Commemorating British and Commonwealth military and civilian servicemen and women's contribution in war and conflict since the end of WWI, this solemn ceremony is held on the Sunday closest to the 11th November, beginning at the time when the armistice was signed in 1918. Two minutes of silence are held at 11am before wreaths are laid at the Cenotaph by the Queen and members of the Royal Family, the Prime Minister, other political leaders and former Prime Ministers, as well as High Commissioners of Commonwealth countries and representatives of the armed forces.

Military bands play live music both before and after the ceremony, and veterans march by the Cenotaph and then back to Horse Guards Parade where a member of the Royal Family takes their salute in front of the Guards Memorial.

Christmas Markets: Hyde Park and the South Bank - November–January

The Christmas Market phenomenon is now an established part of winter celebrations in the capital. An entire section at the south-east of Hyde Park is given over to Winter Wonderland, which seems to grow yearly! This is an enormous festival with stalls selling mulled wine, Christmas fare, clothing, gifts as well as a large skating rink and many thrilling rollercoasters and funfair rides. Families are well catered for too with areas particularly suited to young children. On a cold winter's evening it all seems quite magical and is an excellent place to have fun.

A somewhat smaller, though equally enjoyable festival is held along the Southbank, and like Hyde Park, draws huge crowds, eager to get in the Christmas spirit, buy gifts and sample food from around the world.

SECTION TWO

RIVERSIDE WALK

The walk begins on the north bank of the Thames by the exit to Embankment Underground Station on the Victoria Embankment.

The Embankment is a busy thoroughfare, a major route linking Westminster to the City of London. If you had been standing at this spot about 150 years ago you would not however, have been on dry land! It was a considerably wider River Thames that flowed here at that time; also, a far more polluted body of water. With cholera outbreaks in the early 19th century and the Great Stink of 1858, when the smell rising from the river got so bad that Parliament was seriously considering a move away from the Palace of Westminster, it was decided that London needed a sanitary sewage system. Joseph Bazelgette, Chief Engineer of the Metropolitan Board of Works was commissioned to design the system. In so doing he built sewers beside the north and south sides of the river and then built three embankments to cover them, reclaiming over fifty acres of land from the river upon which the Victoria and Chelsea Embankments (on the north side), and Albert Embankment (on the south side) were constructed.

Until 1750 it had only been possible to cross the Thames by a sole bridge, London Bridge, downstream from here. Since that time many further bridges have been built to accommodate road traffic, pedestrians and the railway. In fact, a project for a new type of bridge is currently under way. This will provide London with a 'Garden Bridge' across the river between the Inns of Court and the South Bank close to the National Theater and will be the first of its kind in the UK.

1. Golden Jubilee Bridge

The bridge we are about to cross is one of two footbridges straddling the Hungerford Railway bridge erected to commemorate HM The Queen's fifty years on the throne in 2002, and now known as the Golden Jubilee Bridge. As you walk along its length there really are some fantastic panoramic views to see of London and you will find many places to stop and take pictures.

At the far end you will see the London Eye over to your right, but take the stairs on your left down to the Riverside Path on the South Bank. Walking eastwards, you will now be alongside one of London's greatest arts and cultural centres, the Southbank Centre.

2. Southbank Centre

Its chief building fronting the river is the Royal Festival Hall, the only legacy still standing from the 1951 Festival of Britain. This was the post-war extravaganza celebration designed to give the British population the feeling of recovery after the austerity of the war years. The Hall has undergone refurbishment several times since then and still remains a wonderful concert venue supporting resident orchestras and artists and is a focus for exhibitions, festivals of music, performance and dance. Its website *www.southbankcentre.co.uk* lists its many activities and will give you up to the minute information about what's on. In addition to the Royal Festival Hall the complex incorporates the Queen Elizabeth Hall and Purcell Room, the Hayward Gallery and Poetry Library.

True to its beginnings as a festival the Southbank Centre hosts many and varied festivals throughout the year that range in themes from African Utopia to Brazilian dance, to Poetry, Literature, a Festival of Love, circus and theater.

During the summer months you can also often attend a free concert or dance performance in one of the Southbank Centre's halls or outside terraces. The Centre has its own bars, café and restaurant, Skylon, as well as an excellent range of restaurants nearby.

3. Skateboard Park

Beneath the Southbank Centre in its undercroft is the renowned skateboarding area. This has been a fundamental attraction for over forty years and distinctive because of its brightly colored graffiti covered walls, ledges and banks. The owners wanted to redevelop the site to create more restaurants and retail outlets here but after an 18-month legal battle the site recently won a reprieve and for the moment at least, is continuing to operate within the South Bank's cultural life.

4. Bookstalls under Waterloo Bridge

This area is very reminiscent of the stalls that line the banks of the River Seine in Paris, and is a great place to browse. Not only selling second-hand books but also many maps and sketches of London and the UK, and the bookstalls stay open every day whatever the weather!

5. British Film Institute (BFI)

Right beside the bookstalls is the BFI with its 4-screen cinemas, and home to the National Archive of Film. Many film seasons are held here during the course of the year. Visitors can view free film and TV from BFI's Mediatheque collections. These include more than 2500 clips from the BFI National Archive collection and range from documentaries to films, children's TV and even home movies, some of which may never have been since first being made! If you are interested in visiting the Mediatheque check on line (*www.bfi.org.uk*) to confirm opening times.

The BFI has its own shop and restaurant (overlooking the Thames) and a first-rate library.

6. The National Theater (*www.nationaltheater.org.uk*)

Just a short stroll from the BFI you reach another arts complex, made up of three permanent theaters, the Olivier, Lyttleton and Dorfman, and one temporary theater. Based in a controversially designed grey concrete building of the 1970s its Brutalist style of architecture is both loved and hated. However, it is hard to decry the views one obtains from its walkways and terraces, especially at sunset when the buildings and parked boats across the river are lit up and everything looks quite magical!

If you have time in your schedule you might like to see a mid-week matinee or an evening performance at the National. The tickets are very reasonably priced, seats are comfortable and all afford good views of the stage. It is easy to reserve tickets on-line or buy them from the Box Office inside the theater complex.

Theater lovers might also be interested in joining a Backstage Tour when much is revealed about what goes on behind the scenes in staging over 20 productions each year.

7. The River Thames, the Thames path and sand artists

Although you can stroll right beside the river today, and it is something that locals and tourists take for granted this has not always been possible. Since Roman times the south side of the river was a marshy, boggy and somewhat isolated area. However, the arrival of the Industrial Revolution in the 18th and 19th centuries saw great changes as the landscape altered entirely, with the introduction of wharves, quaysides, railways, individual factories and manufacturing premises. Unsurprisingly, densely packed housing soon followed as people wanted to live beside their places of work, and in time these became slum-like in character.

The enormous damage caused by bombing on either side of the river during WWII left the area even more scarred, but the destruction acted as a catalyst for regeneration which has continued ever since.

The cultural and arts centres already passed by on the walk are excellent examples of this, and the establishment of the pedestrianized Thames river path in recent years is really a wonderful addition, making it so much more accessible to the public. What could be better that enjoying London from the riverside, watching the ebb and flow of the Thames approximately twice a day, with its range of up to 8 m (26 ft) from high-tide to low-tide.

The river is so much an integral and significant part of London – for many years the prime transport route and London's artery, and there is something very pleasing about sitting at a bench and watching the river, its traffic and the world go by.

Just beneath the path is the Thames shoreline with its many beaches. This is where, at low-tide, you will see people scavenging for 'treasure' sometimes using metal detectors. It is even known for some of the finds (coins, jewellery, 16th century bricks, and clay pipes) to reach their way into the Museum of London! On the beach in front of Gabriel's Wharf by the Oxo Tower, is 'Ernie's beach' named after a local resident and activist who has campaigned relentlessly to retain the Thames foreshore and prevent it from being swallowed up by development. Sand artists are frequently seen here building works of art and entertaining the crowds who look on from behind the railings above. It is not unusual for cartoon characters to be drawn, or even models of furniture such as settees, tables and chairs.

Ernie's beach, Gabriel's Wharf and the Oxo Tower, are all administered by a co-operative association, the Coin Street Community Builders (CSCB), established in 1984. Threatened with the likelihood of a huge office development in the 1980s the local residents banded together to save the 13-acre site and obtained planning permission to re-generate it. They built co-operative housing, art galleries, boutiques, eateries, the Bernie Spain Gardens, Gabriel's Wharf and a riverside walkway. Due to its eclectic mix of shops, culture and cuisine the area is always brimming with life and many events and festivals take place here throughout the year.

8. Gabriel's Wharf and the Oxo Tower

Apart from being a convenient spot to grab a drink, meal or snack, Gabriel's Wharf is filled with small boutiques selling handicrafts, jewellery, art and clothing in an interesting setting. More shops can be found just a little further along the path at the Oxo Tower Wharf. Here, you'll encounter art galleries (Bargehouse and gallery@oxo) exhibition spaces, cafes, fashion and design shops and studios on the ground and first floor level of the famous Oxo Tower.

The building itself dates back to the late 19th century when it was constructed

as a power station but in the 1920s was bought up by the Liebig Extract of Meat Company who produced the Oxo beef stock cubes. The company had the building largely re-built in the new art deco style and converted into a cold store. To advertise their product Liebig intended to raise illuminated signs on a tower facing the river but at the time such skyline advertising was prohibited. To get around the 'problem' the company built a tower and included at the top a design of a circle, a cross and a circle, spelling out OXO, the name of the stock cube.

Today, the building remains one of London's major river landmarks, and is particularly celebrated for its restaurant and brasserie and outstanding river views. Naturally, it is a pricey though very popular venue to eat but if you just want to see the view there is a free observation gallery located on the terrace beside the Brasserie on the 8th floor.

9. Bankside Gallery

Opposite the Founders Arms pub is a surprisingly less well-known exhibition space, the gallery of the Royal Watercolor Society and the Royal Society of Painter-Printmakers, Bankside Gallery. Free, and open daily during exhibitions, the gallery exists to promote watercolor and original print through exhibitions of the artists of the two royal societies that date back to the 19th century. It has a small shop within selling some unusual greeting cards as well as books specialising in art techniques.

10. Tate Modern gardens/riverside

At this point in the walk you may want to stop for a snack or simply sit for a while in the gardens outside Tate Modern. The area lends itself to people watching and it is relaxing looking at the boats on the river and enjoying the views. Drinks and food are available at the Founders Arms pub and also within Tate Modern at its level I café or in the river-front restaurant on level 6.

11. Bankside

Leave Tate Modern and continue your walk past the Millennium Bridge and Shakespeare's Globe Theater alongside the river. Four centuries ago this was a road beside the river wall lined with 22 inns all of which have long since gone except the Anchor, which you will reach in a while. In the early 1600s the Globe was one of four theaters in the area, the others being the Swan, the Hope and the Rose, but all had disappeared by the time of the Interregnum (1649–1660) when the Puritans lead by Oliver Cromwell were governing the country.

   As you step into the tunnel beneath Southwark Bridge you will see some fascinating wall murals illustrating London's first Frost Fair in 1564, which took place on the frozen River Thames. At that time the river was broader and flowed less fast, hampered by Old London Bridge with its 19 arches. Although the river no longer freezes Bankside continues this tradition and hosts an annual winter

Frost Fair, a popular festival full of market stalls, music and theater.

Continue walking past the Anchor pub, one of Bankside's few remaining ancient inns and where in 1666 Samuel Pepys sat watching his city burn down. The present building dates to 1775 and is said to be where Samuel Johnson wrote his dictionary in rented rooms. Follow the cobbled stone path and on your right you will shortly pass the Clink prison tourist attraction.

In Tudor times, the whole district known as Bankside was teeming with people, especially after dark when it came into its own as a major entertainments centre outside of the jurisdiction of the City fathers (authorities). To all intents and purposes it was the playground of the City of London at this time, known for its bull, dog and bear-baiting, its cock-pits, theaters and prostitutes. The Bishop of Winchester, a most important and influential figure as well as a clergyman, had his London residence beside the river and responsibility for controlling and licensing the district's brothels came under his jurisdiction. He would mete out punishments in his own courts and prison (The Clink). Londoners seeking entertainment would arrive at Bankside by boat and pass many an evening of debauchery enjoying the delights of the riverside.

In a moment you will pass by the ruins of the Bishop's palace on the right (It is worth stopping here to look at its beautiful rose window), just before you reach the replica of Sir Francis Drake's galleon, The Golden Hinde II. Drake had circumnavigated the globe in his Elizabethan vessel between 1577–1580. This boat, moored in St Mary Overie Dock took to the seas some 200 years later in the 1970s and like Drake's original undertook a 225,000 km (140,000 mi) sea journey stopping at over 300 ports on the way. Today it has become a popular tourist attraction with costumed actors and interactive tours and is open 10am–5.30pm daily.

Shortly you will reach a junction where the path veers right. This marks the end of your riverside walk and Southwark Cathedral is directly in front of you.

SOUTHWARK CATHEDRAL

Familiar for its soaring roof tower and Medieval features, the 12th century Cathedral is the earliest Gothic church in the whole of London. Despite being less well-known than St Paul's Cathedral or Westminster Abbey, it too has a

wealth of history and a beautiful interior.

Built on the site of a Roman villa, a 7th century convent and a Saxon monasterium, the church is located at the west end of London Bridge which between the 12th and 18th centuries was the only crossing and link between the City of London and Bankside.

In the Tudor period this was Shakespeare's parish church; he lived nearby working at the Globe Theater and it is where his brother Edmund is buried. Within the Cathedral Shakespeare is remembered in a memorial and a window that depicts characters from a number of his plays.

Contemporaries of Shakespeare, Philip Massinger and John Fletcher lie buried here as does Lawrence Fletcher, co-lessee of the Globe Theater.

Of particular note is the Harvard Chapel commemorating John Harvard. John, born into a local wealthy family was baptized in 1607 at St Saviour's Church (now Southwark Cathedral). He remained a parishioner here until he and his wife emigrated to America in the 1630s, after acquiring much of his family fortune.

On his death in 1638 he bequeathed half of his estate towards the establishment of a college and from this was born Harvard University. He gifted his valuable library too and so the university remembers its London benefactor with great affection.

In 2012 a new window was installed within the Cathedral to mark the sixty years that HM The Queen has been on the throne. Designed by Icelandic painter and stained glass artist Leifur Breidfjord, it is a very vivid eye-catching window that complements the other stained glass windows at the east end of the church.

The Cathedral is particularly renowned for its music and if you are here at the start of the week you might well catch its Monday lunchtime organ recital or Tuesday afternoon recital. In summer you can also often hear live music outside in the churchyard. Go to *www.southwark.anglican.org* for the most up to date information about its music programme and events.

BOROUGH MARKET

A visit to Borough Market is a fabulous way to round off your day of sightseeing. If you're passionate about eating and drinking or just enjoy looking at marvelous and tempting displays of produce then this is the place to be!

Nestled under the arches of the railway above at London Bridge Station, the market is always colorful and full of life. Major market days are Friday and Saturday but many stalls are open from Wednesday, and some even open on other days too (though the entire market is closed on Sunday).

The stalls selling meat, fish, cheese, fruit, vegetables, wine and beer are often run by the producers themselves. They are not only highly knowledgeable about their produce but also willing to answer questions and to give hints and advice as to how best to keep and cook their food. With such a reputation it is not surprising that chefs and restauranteurs from all over London come to the

market to purchase food and drink for their establishments.

In fact, times have moved little over the past 1000 years; records show that there was a market in the Borough of Southwark that sold meat and produce as early as 1014, and even then it attracted buyers from throughout London and its outlying districts. By the 19th century, when London's docks were at their busiest and great quantities of food were imported by ship, the area around London Bridge became known as 'London's Larder', and the market thrived.

Nowadays, there is much emphasis on organic and high quality foodstuffs and the market is full of mouth-watering lunchtime food stalls as well as bars and cafes, ideal for a light lunch or snack. The market remains one of the only two wholesale markets still operating in central London today (Smithfield, near the City, being the other).

Fans of the 'Bridget Jones' films might recognize the Globe pub beside the market, as it was here, above the pub that Bridget lived.

THE GEORGE INN – BOROUGH HIGH STREET

Two minutes walk away from the market you step back into the Elizabethan age at the George Inn which is a real icon and the last of its type within London. A galleried pub and coaching inn, the George was once one of several in the area, the most famous of which perhaps is the Tabard Inn from where in 1388 Geoffrey Chaucer began 'The Canterbury Tales'.

Sadly, only the south face of the Inn is left standing today and the pub shares its yard with rather ugly looking 20th century office buildings. Even so, it still retains an atmosphere of times gone by and if you have read Charles Dickens' 'Little Dorrit' you should recognize its name.

Such inns were common in the 1600s and it is believed that they were the forerunners of the theaters. Actors performed on a platform within the courtyard and would be surrounded by the audience. For a better view you would pay a premium and stand in the Galleries. Monies for the entertainment would be collected at an office at the front of the yard, which became known as the 'Box Office'.

Nowadays, the George Inn is owned by the National Trust (a charitable body that preserves British heritage and buildings), leased out and run entirely as a pub. However, originally it would have had bedrooms where travelers would have stayed after a long, and most probably, uncomfortable coach journey. The downstairs, with its uneven well-trodden floors consists of a number of connecting rooms and is both quaint and extremely atmospheric.

The pub still uses all these rooms and offers a good and wide selection of British seasonal food (sandwiches, pies, grills, burgers and salads) plus an excellent range of beers. The main restaurant is situated on the 1st floor from where you get a very good view of the historic galleried section and can enjoy the atmosphere of the ancient 17th century inn. In winter-time mulled wine is sold and fires are lit around the bars, conjuring up life in Dickensian London.

When you leave The George turn right into Borough High Street and you will see London Bridge underground station about 100 m (325 ft) ahead (*Northern and Jubilee lines*).

PICTURE CAPTIONS

1 - Somerset House Fountains

2 - Shakespeare's Globe Theater

3 - Millennium Bridge and St Paul's Cathedral

4 - National Theater on the South Bank

5 - Southbank Centre and beach

6 - Oxo Tower and Riverside

7 - Southwark Cathedral. Shakespeare's Window

8 - Southwark Cathedral. Memorial to Shakespeare

9 - Borough Market

DAY 5 SHOPPING AND CULTURE IN THE WEST END

SECTION ONE

FROM OXFORD STREET TO THE NATIONAL GALLERY

OXFORD STREET

This is probably one of the world's busiest shopping streets, full of well-known international shops and department stores. Being in the heart of the West End and well served by bus and tube (it has four underground stations along its length), it is not hard to understand its popularity. Its shops open weekdays between 9am–10am in the morning closing around 8pm–9pm. Sunday opening has been restricted by law since the 1990s which results in busy trading throughout the day, with larger stores opening 12pm–6pm and smaller shops, 11am-5pm.

Marble Arch tube station brings you to the far west of Oxford Street and it is a short walk from here to Selfridges. This is one of London's great shopping emporiums and the only store in the world to have been voted three times 'Best Department Store in the World'. At the cutting edge of retail since American Harry Gordon Selfridge established his store in 1909, Selfridges is famous for its impressive food hall, its variety and extent of brands, and for offering both designer clothes and high street fashion in just one building! Arranged over 6 floors plus a roof terrace, the store is filled to the rafters with appealing merchandise and its distinctive yellow bags are a must-have souvenir!

Harry Gordon Selfridge (1858–1947) was both an entrepreneur and innovator wanting to provide customers with something extra, the like of which they had never experienced before. Having arrived in London in 1906, already a wealthy man, he bought a site in Oxford Street which he developed into a department store and opened with great celebration in 1909 following an exciting advertising campaign. A real showman he introduced a programme of special events pulling in crowds of shoppers throughout his thirty-year-plus leadership of the store. Selfridge himself was an extremely charismatic and utterly charming man and was totally committed to giving the very best service to his customers. He worked and played hard enjoying the most extravagant lifestyle, entertaining lavishly and surrounding himself with women after the death of his wife in 1918. The years of the recession together with his addiction to gambling and expensive women left him practically penniless and he ultimately left the store in 1941. However, his vision of a department store with the most advanced standards in retailing has endured and Selfridges remains to this day at the very front of its field. The present owners continue to develop and expand Selfridges ensuring that a visit here is indeed an exceptional shopping experience.

Three more department stores, Debenhams, The House of Fraser and John Lewis are close to Bond Street Station and here too shoppers will find a wide selection of goods in their many departments. John Lewis's policy of being 'Never Knowingly Undersold' means that if you buy a product here and find the same item cheaper elsewhere, they will refund the difference; a great slogan and very popular with its loyal customer base.

Beside the tube station, around Oxford Circus, at the junction where Oxford Street and Regent Street meet there are a cluster of high street shops such as TopShop, H&M, TopMan, New Look, Zara, Urban Outfitters and Mango. From here down to Tottenham Court Road Station at its far end you can shop at many other mainstream shops, including Marks and Spencer (M&S), one of the UK's oldest and much loved clothing and food chains. The store started out over 130 years ago as a Penny Bazaar market stall in the north of England and established a reputation for selling quality goods from the start. This Oxford Street store is one of its largest and carries a great selection of lingerie and cashmere tops and sweaters. Towards the end of the street close to the tube you will reach a very large Primark (the cut-price fashion store) always packed with shoppers and a great favourite with young people.

Re-trace your steps to Oxford Circus, and turn left by the tube into Regent Street.

REGENT STREET, CARNABY STREET AND SAVILE ROW

Regent Street, like Oxford Street is lined with shops, some designer, some specialist. One of Apple's flagship stores is situated right by Oxford Circus and always crammed full of people trying out the latest Apple iPhones, computers and tablets. Across the road about a block further down on the corner of Great Marlborough Street you reach Liberty, which is housed in one of the most prominent Tudor revival Arts and Crafts buildings in London. Intimate in feel it is decorated with oak wood panelling, beams, wooden balconies, carved oak panels and stained glass. A unique building with its own distinctive style

its Tudor wing is clad with timbers taken from two of the UK's last wooden naval ships (HMS Impregnable and HMS Hindustan). Liberty's is famous first and foremost for its fabrics and textiles but it also offers an excellent and wide selection of merchandise ranging from clothing to home ware and stationery, bags, scarves and travel accessories.

Just around the corner from the store is another landmark mainly associated with Swinging London of the 1960s, **Carnaby Street.** Then the hub of London's fashion streets it was full of small boutiques and famous names such as Mary Quant, Lady Jane, Irvine Sellars and Lord John. At the time Carnaby Street was one of the coolest places to be seen and was famed for its Hippie and Mod styles attracting huge numbers of visitors. Pop groups and their followers hung out here and John Stephen was where Mods went to get their clothes. Stephen, sometimes referred to as 'The King of Carnaby Street', also kitted out the Beatles, Rolling Stones, Small Faces and Jimi Hendrix. Even in later

decades Carnaby Street was where punks and goths bought their clothing.

Nowadays, although very much a fashion enclave the shops tend to be less 'fringe' than in the past. Instead you'll find the likes of North Face, Levi's, Vans and American Apparel, plus a selection of small designer shops and eateries in the three floor Kingly Court which you discover through an opening off the street.

Carnaby Street these days is pedestrianized and easy to find by its somewhat kitsch archway! Very much part of the West End fashion scene and on the edge of Soho, it is still an interesting area to visit.

Moments away from here on Regent Street you will find yourself transported into an entirely different world, the magical world of Hamley's, London's major children's store. With seven floors bursting with every type of toy, game, board game and stuffed animal on the market, the store cannot be missed! Here you find areas dedicated to soft toys and teddy bears, dolls, train sets, action toys and electronic games. At any time of the year Hamley's is full of bustle and noise whilst children wonder at the choice available and plead with their parents to buy everything in sight! Undoubtedly, Christmas is the best time to visit when the store is full to the rafters and Hamley's window displays captivate and enchant both young and old alike.

Regent Street was actually planned as a shopping street in the 1820s. The architect, John Nash, promised the Prince Regent (later King George IV), to build a wide and grand thoroughfare connecting the newly developed Regent's Park sited to the north of Oxford Street with the Prince's mansion, Carlton House about a mile or so away (near to where Buckingham Palace is sited today). Although many of the original buildings no longer exist the street has retained much of its former character and has thus attracted many internationally renowned shops such as Jaegar, Austin Reed, Burberry, Aquascutum and Mango. Parallel to Regent Street on its west side is **Savile Row**, home since the late 1700s to hand and individually made gentlemen's suits and clothing, and more recently to the US retailer Abercrombie and Fitch. Apart from its reputation for tailoring Savile Row has links with royalty, the rich and the famous attracting customers such as world leaders, military men, pop stars and actors from throughout the globe.

As you pass by look closely at these shops for many of them have shields on their windows or above the doorway. These are **Royal Warrants** granted to tradesmen who supply HRH The Queen, HRH The Duke of Edinburgh or HRH The Prince of Wales as a mark of recognition. To qualify for a royal warrant the trader must have supplied products regularly to royalty and for a period of five years out of seven and furthermore may receive separate warrants from each of the three members of the Royal Family. There are a number of regulations that apply and they are strictly adhered to. Royal Warrant holders are entitled to use the legend 'By Appointment' and display the Royal Arms on their products, on their delivery vehicles, stationery and advertising material. There are currently about 800 Royal Warrant Holders throughout the UK.

THE NATIONAL GALLERY AND NATIONAL PORTRAIT GALLERY

Not only does the National Gallery look imposing as it sits on the north terrace above Trafalgar Square but it also is home to the most impressive collection of artwork, some of which is priceless. Its four wings display masterpieces of the greatest painters of the time and of the main European schools between 1250 and 1900. The newest building, to the west of the main entrance, The Sainsbury Wing, houses the oldest paintings, so if you want to visit the artwork chronologically you should start your tour here.

It is probably advisable to look at the Gallery website *www.thenationalgallery. org.uk* before you arrive as it has a good deal of useful information and may help you to prepare for your visit. The Gallery's collection is small (2,300) when compared with some other European art galleries but nearly every painting is a major work of art and the artists are renowned throughout the world. From Botticelli's 'Venus and Mars', Da Vinci's, 'The Virgin of the Rocks', Titian's 'Bacchus and Ariadne' to Hans Holbein the Younger's, 'The Ambassadors', Diego Velasquez's 'The Rokeby Venus', Rembrandt's 'Self-Portraits', Hogarth's 'Marriage a la Mode' and JWW Turner's 'The Fighting Temeraire' every picture is a real masterpiece! In addition the Gallery displays much Impressionist work showing the art of Manet, Monet, Seurat, Cezanne and Van Gogh.

Exploring the Gallery you will find paintings from 1500–1600 in the West Wing, from–1700 in the North Wing, and the remaining collection covering 1700–1900, in the East Wing.

Daily guided tours lasting an hour are held at am and 2.30pm (with extra tours run on weekends). If you don't have much time you may want to attend one of the Gallery's free lunchtime talks which take place at 1pm for about 45 minutes. Short ten minute talks are also given at 4pm Monday–Friday.

To enhance your visit to the Gallery there is a free podcast that can be downloaded, and (for a small charge) a variety of Audio Tours can be hired, an excellent way to find out more about the National Gallery's wonderful collection.

There are three eating places, a restaurant, café and espresso bar in the Gallery and several shops in the main entrance, at the Sainsbury wing and the Getty entrance. These all stock a wide selection of books, gifts, postcards and posters.

Late night opening at the Gallery takes place on Friday when the Gallery closes at 9pm.

The original collection dates back to 1824 and was purchased by Parliament from banker John Julius Angerstein. As it grew in size it moved in the late 1830s to its present site, the former King's Mews and stables, and continued its expansion in the course of the 20th century. Similar to London's other free entry museums and art galleries, the National Gallery runs frequent exhibitions during the year for which an admission fee is charged.

If you are coming to London and know you want to see an exhibition here that is likely to be a blockbuster it makes sense to buy your tickets on-line in advance.

National Portrait Gallery

Beside the National Gallery is another gem of a museum, the National Portrait Gallery, which as its name suggests is a collection of portraits of famous men and women, from the 16th century to present day. Here you find superb paintings, miniatures, photographs, sculptures, and drawings of monarchs, statesmen, celebrities, writers, scientists and artists. The top floor galleries cover early English kings along with the Tudors, Stuarts and Hanoverians (up to 1837) and lower floors focus on portraits since the reign of Queen Victoria.

Contemporary 20th and 21st century portraits are displayed on the ground floor. Also on this floor temporary exhibitions are held in the Wolfson and Porter Galleries. Audio guides in six languages, highlighting key portraits within the collection, are available from the Information Desk in the Main Hall for which a small charge is made. For families a further audio guide is available containing 4 tours for children aged 7–11.

The gallery is open daily from 10am–6pm and remains open until 9pm on Thursday–Friday when the museum offers a programme of events with live music (Friday), a bar, talks and workshops.

For a wonderful view over Westminster make your way to the roof-top restaurant/bar or if you are looking for gifts visit the gallery shops where you will find prints, books and postcards.

SKY-HIGH RESTAURANTS, THEMED BARS AND

HISTORIC LONDON PUBS

Since the very first establishment in the 1960s of London's revolving restaurant at the Post Office Tower (now the BT Tower) Londoners and visitors have been accustomed to dining from a height.

Today, it almost seems that the sky-high dining experience is practically commonplace! With a city full of towering glass edifices, high-rise hotels, lofty museums, department stores and pubs with their own roof terraces we have the perfect locations for dining under the stars and enjoying wonderful panoramic views.

The Shard, 87 storeys high and London's tallest building has a superb range of restaurants and cocktail bars located between its 31st and 52nd floors, all of which give magnificent views day and night.

On the opposite bank of the Thames in the Square Mile there are even more places to enjoy a sunset, fine dining and cocktails from up high: **Tower 42**, by Bank junction, **20 Fenchurch Street** (aka, The Walkie Talkie), the **Heron Tower**

in Bishopsgate, are all very popular venues, not somewhere to go for a quick cheap drink, yet certainly difficult to beat for the view. You can also visit **Madison's** on the roof of One New Change, great for cocktails and end of work drinks.

Tower Bridge hires its

walkways as a venue for dining, parties and even weddings and has to be one of London's most fairy-tale settings. High above the Thames you can now see down to the bridge through its glass floor as well as look out along the river at the many London's sights.

Roof-top bars and dining

These have become extremely more fashionable in London. Each summer **Selfridges** in the West End opens a roof-top bar and restaurant and introduces a new theme. Most recently it was kitted out as a seaside resort with fishing nets, beach balls, seaside huts and even deck chairs.

The **Roof Gardens**, is a fabulous 7th floor venue in the heart of High Street Kensington. With its club (open Friday and Saturday nights), restaurant, stunning gardens and rooftop views it is a great place to enjoy London.

Themed Bars

This is another area that has grown dramatically in recent times and there is now a real diversity of bars in town. In Kensington High Street is **Bodo's Schloss**, an Austrian ski lodge, equipped with Alpine restaurant, bar and nightclub, and where the staff all wear lederhosen and dirndl skirts. **Bounce** and **Ping** (Holborn and Earl's Court) are two bars that cater for ping-pong players; **Bar Kick** (Shoreditch) is similar but offers table football tables, whilst **Swingers** in Shoreditch and **Plonk** in Dalston have crazy-golf courses. South of the Thames in Vauxhall you can combine roller-skating with a drinking session at the **Renaissance Rooms** whilst back in the West End a visit to the **Absolut Icebar** (off Regent Street) allows you to drink in an environment where the walls, furniture, bars and even your glass are all made from Norwegian river ice! If you prefer a warmer setting then karaoke is the main selling point of **Karaoke Box** in Smithfield and Soho.

Historic and interesting pubs

Throughout London you will come across historic and traditional pubs which conjure up life in times gone by. **The George Inn** in Borough High Street certainly gives an idea of what a 16th century coaching inn would have been like, and there are wonderful examples of Victorian drinking halls dotted all over central London and in the suburbs.

Go to Little Venice to see two fine examples of beautiful and rather special 19th century pubs; the **Prince Alfred**, near to Warwick Avenue tube, is a delightful Grade I listed building with a tiled mosaic entranceway and fabulously ornate ceiling. Its five tiny bars are separated by etched glass and carved mahogany. Just up the road you reach the **Warrington Hotel**, also a listed building, with original stained glass windows, mosaic floors and the most impressive marble fireplace.

Similarly ornate Victorian pubs can be found in Oxford Circus, at the **Argyll Arms**, and the **Salisbury**, on St Martin's Lane right in the middle of the theater district.

In Wapping, east of the Tower of London, is the **Prospect of Whitby**, reputedly dating back to 1520, although it has undergone a number of refurbishments over the centuries!

A short trip north to Hampstead will bring you to the wonderfully atmospheric 16th century **Spaniards Inn**, reputedly a haunt of highwaymen, written about by Charles Dickens in 'Pickwick Papers' and possibly where John Keats wrote his 'Ode to a Nightingale'.

Back in central London you are really spoilt for choice as there are so many interesting and welcoming pubs. Fleet Street's **Ye Olde Cheshire Cheese** is certainly worth a visit. Re-built following the Great Fire of London in 1666 it is entered through a side alleyway and appears to be quite small. Yet, it fills several floors and has many wood-panelled bars built on a number of levels. In the 18th and 19th centuries it was the regular hangout for many literary figures such as Sir Arthur Conan Doyle, Mark Twain, Dr Samuel Johnson, and Charles Dickens and it remains well-frequented even today.

As you walk through the small alleyways in the nearby Square Mile you will find at many a twist and turn a small opening leading to an unexpected pub. Quite often such pubs will only open between Monday and Friday when the City is full of workers, closing over the weekend when the City is quieter. An excellent pub/restaurant in this area is **Simpson's Tavern**, which provides breakfasts and lunch and then shuts for the day. Founded in 1757 it claims to be the oldest chop house in London and until 1916 women were not allowed in its premises! Situated in Ball Court off Cornhill, it stands opposite another famous watering hole, now known as **Jamaica Wine House**, but which opened as London's first coffee shop by Pasque Rosee during the 16th century.

SECTION TWO

LUXURY SHOPPING, CULTURE AND AFTERNOON TEA

GENTLEMAN'S LONDON

Most probably on a first visit to London you will have spent some time in the West End shopping in Oxford Street and Regent Street. Quite possibly you discovered and browsed in the Waterstone's flagship bookstore or its older neighbour, Hatchard's on Piccadilly, but rarely will visitors stumble upon the enclave of gentlemen's shops and clubs in the vicinity of St James's Palace, affectionately known as 'Gentleman's London'.

Located between Piccadilly in the north and Pall Mall to the south, this area developed from about the late 17th century when many Londoners moved west out of the City of London following the Great Fire of 1666. New housing was rapidly built and this is turn lead to a requirement for shops. Being so close to St James's Palace the local residents tended to be courtiers or nobles and aristocrats and so it was that shops selling goods such as hunting supplies, tobacco, men's grooming ware, fine wines, everyday and formal clothing and evening attire became established there.

St James's Street, off Piccadilly is where you will find two such shops. The first, **Lock & Co Ltd,** towards the end of the street on the left, has been manufacturing gentlemen's hats since 1676. Not only one of the oldest family businesses to exist it is also the oldest hat shop in the world! Celebrated for providing hats for statesmen and naval and military leaders like Sir Winston Churchill, Admiral Nelson and the Duke of Wellington it is also renowned for its 'Bowler' hat, a hard felt hat with a rounded crown, worn originally by the working classes in Victorian times but later popular with the middle and upper classes. From the early 20th century the bowler hat was almost part of a 'uniform' worn by men working in the City of London along with a rolled umbrella! Nowadays Lock and Co's range of hats on offer is enormous, one for every occasion and for all types of weather. You will find panama and straw hats, top hats, trilbys, tweed, leather, fur hats, the list is endless! Although initially a shop for gentlemen alone Locks now provides for ladies too, offering both traditional and fashionable headwear of the very best quality to people of every age and background. As a shop used by both HRH the Prince of Wales and HRH the Duke of Edinburgh it is the proud holder of royal warrants (See Section I above).

Just a few doors along from Locks is the wine merchants **Berry Bros and Rudd**, which has occupied these premises for over 300 years! As Britain's oldest wine and spirit merchant the store has supplied royalty for much of that period and has always served the rich and famous including Lord Byron and the Aga Khan. Like Locks the business is still owned and run by members of the Berry and Rudd families.

Both shops exist in the shadow of St James's Palace and would have benefited from the proximity to the Court in the early years of their trading. Their clientele then, as now, spent much time in the coffee shops and clubs that grew up nearby. Many **gentlemen's clubs** are still based around St James's Street and Pall Mall, but you might not know it, as they are very discreet and there is nothing to

advertise their existence outside their buildings. However, St James's Street is home to White's, Boodle's and Brooks's, and Pall Mall to the Athenaeum, Traveller's, Reform, Oxford and Cambridge, and RAC clubs, the latter being famous for its luxurious Egyptian style basement swimming pool. If you are lucky enough to gain entry (you will need to accompany a club member) you will understand why membership is so coveted. The clubs are wonderfully spacious and comfortable and all have bars and wonderful dining facilities. Most offer accommodation too (often very competitive if not cheaper than central London hotels), so an attractive place to meet with friends and colleagues and an overnight stay. Until fairly recently, the clubs were purely a gentleman's domain but since the equality legislation of the 1970s this has mainly changed and now most clubs allow both entry and membership to women, although some still prohibit women from using some of the club's rooms and bars!

Towards the end of the 18th century the interest in clothing and fashion became very intense when the dandy, **George 'Beau' Brummell** (1778–1840) became

popular. Brummell, initially a close friend of the Prince Regent (the future King George IV), was renowned both for his eccentric ways – he washed himself for two hours daily before dressing (at a time when this was uncommon), and for his care in his appearance and his truly fastidious dress sense, believing in the best, though simple tailoring.

When he finished his elaborate preparations and finally left the house he would travel by sedan chair so as not to dirty his shoes or be subject to the vagaries of the weather when his hair or clothing might be blown about by the wind or rain! In **Jermyn Street**, the very heart of Gentleman's London, you will find a superb bronze statue of Brummell just in front of the Piccadilly Arcade. It shows him beautifully attired sporting a cravat, coat, top boots and carrying a top hat, most probably a purchase from nearby Lock's. He was a real celebrity of the day whose style was emulated by his many fans.

Further along this street and those that radiate from it are many high-end luxury gentlemen's outfitters. Today, City gents visiting their clubs in the area are often seen entering one of the traditional specialist shops like the perfumery Floris (in its premises since 1730), Hawes & Curtis which sells gentlemen's high quality and stylish clothing, George F Trumper, barber and perfumer, and Paxton & Whitfield cheesemongers. Favourbrook is a newer 20th century addition to Jermyn Street but has become fashionable all the same offering less conventional though highly elegant and well-tailored male clothing.

Fortnum and Mason

Also adorned with Royal Warrants, this beautifully elegant store sandwiched between Piccadilly and Jermyn Street, has to be the icing on the cake of your visit to the area.

It too has an entire floor dedicated to and catering for traditional gentlemen's requirements, but the store itself began its life in the early 1700s as a small shop selling provisions and is still recognized for its great variety of quality and exclusive groceries over three centuries later!

William Fortnum was a footman to Queen Anne. His partner, Hugh Mason, ran a small store in St James's Market, and deciding to join forces, they began their business in 1707. In the Royal Household it was Fortnum's job each night to replenish candles used by the palace, and he was able to re-sell the partly-used candles. In selling the candle stumps as well as some groceries he developed an enterprise becoming the Queen's grocer, and his shop became 'the biggest tuck-box in the world'. It was not until 1773 however, that the business was established on its present site.

During the mid 18th century, there was an explosion in trade. This in turn created a middle class, affluent and willing to spend their money. International trade also expanded dramatically as new routes were discovered and transport became more reliable, with London at the hub of everything making it a magnet for the world. Fortnum & Mason (Fortnum's) was right at the centre of this whirlwind. There were strong links with the British East India Company (almost an independent imperial power with its own policies, and army), and this paved the way for Fortnum's to become an emporium for goods sold nowhere else!

For about fifty years at the end of the 18th century Fortnum's acted as a 'Post Office'. It had letterboxes for paid/unpaid letters that were picked up 6 times a day. Soldiers and sailors, already among the company's best customers, received a discount! This meant that every type of customer was attracted to the store, and ever more tempted by the wonderful interior and window displays.

By the 1780s Fortnum's was selling mince pies and food in aspic, and by the turn of the century it was well established as the premier supplier of exotic edibles to the gentry! In the early 1800s, a new department was opened to cater for gentlemen's clubs such as the Athenaeum and Boodles. It even sent provisions to Captain Scott in the Antarctic in the early 20th century!

Fortnum's first hampers appeared in 1788 consisting of such delicacies as lobster and game pies for shooting parties and supplying provisions to busy MP's. By now they were famous for their ready-to-eat luxury foods, e.g. West

Indian Turtle for 10 shillings a pound, and exotic foods (boar's head, mangoes, truffles). The Fortnum's hampers were abundant at all the 'social' occasions: Henley, Wimbledon, The Boat Race, Ascot, Lord's and Twickenham.

From the middle of the 19th century the store sold tinned food, but was the first in 1886 to take on tins from an American entrepreneur called Heinz. This was the start of the British love of 'Baked Beans'!

You can still purchase a Fortnum's hamper as well as tea, coffee, jams, biscuits, chocolates and the most enormous selection of exotic groceries on its ground and basement floors. One thing is for certain, you are unlikely to leave without having bought something from the Food Hall, packed full of such tempting and beautifully packaged provisions.

Exit the store by the Piccadilly doorway and then cross the road. Look back at the store façade and you will see the Fortnum's clock above the entrance. Only a relatively recent addition (1964) its bells originate from the same foundry as those of Big Ben. Stand here when the hour strikes and you get to see Messrs Fortnum and Mason appear, checking that standards are being kept in the store they began!

High up on the roof the store now has its own colonies of bees. These are lodged in 2 m (6.5 ft) high beehives each painted in Fortnum's Eau-de-Nil signature shade with a triumphal arch entrance and copper-clad pagoda roofs in four different styles: Mughal, Roman, Chinese and Gothick. The honey from the hives is for sale within the store.

THE ROYAL ACADEMY OF ARTS

The Royal Academy of Arts sits in Burlington House just off Piccadilly. The magnificent 18th century mansion is enclosed within its own courtyard set back from the hustle and bustle of the road. Designed for Lord Burlington by Colen Campbell in the Palladian style, it is almost palatial and a splendid example of this Italian inspired architecture.

The Royal Academy, established in 1768 is led by its members, leading artists, sculptors and architects, known as Royal Academicians (RA). Some current members include Anthony Caro, Cornelia Parker, Richard Long, Anthony Gormley, Tacita Dean, Richard Rogers, Norman Foster and Zaha Hadid. On being elected to the Academy each has given a piece of their work to its collection which accounts for the Royal Academy's amazing breadth of objects, masterpieces and installations.

The members elect their President from amongst their number and this role has been carried out by many eminent artists since the Academy was formed in the 18th century including Edwin Lutyens, Sir Thomas Lawrence, Lord Leighton and American Benjamin West. A statue of the first president, Joshua Reynolds stands in the centre of the courtyard.

The Royal Academy was Britain's first formal art school, a role that is very much at the core of its existence today.

Within the building it displays a wide range of artwork; photographs, paintings, architectural designs, sculptures and drawings. Highlights of the permanent collection are found in the John Madejski Fine Rooms, a very fine suite of 18th century State Rooms on the first floor, and in the more recent Sackler Galleries extension designed by Norman Foster in 1991. Here, you will see one of the treasures of the Royal Academy, the Taddei Tondo, the marble sculpture by Michelangelo of the Virgin and Child with the infant St John (1504–5).

The Royal Academy regularly puts on an exciting exhibitions programme displaying art and architecture from the ancient world to contemporary art and installations. In recent years its exhibitions have included The Real Van Gogh, David Hockney RA, German artist Anselm Kiefer, Rubens and his legacy, Anish Kapoor, Giovanni Batista Moroni and Ai Weiwei, one of China's most eminent and important artists.

The Summer Exhibition is probably the most famous of all the Royal Academy's events and has been held annually without interruption since the institution began in 1769. It brings together about 1,200 contemporary works of art and displays them all throughout Burlington House for a two month period. The works are submitted by both new and established artists, the artworks selected accounting for only about a tenth of those put forward to the Selection and Hanging Committee of the Academy. A great number of the works are for sale allowing you to buy the art of emerging as well as known artists. During the Summer Exhibition artists may also win prizes and awards for their work in a variety of categories: photography, painting, sculpture, architecture and drawing.

The Royal Academy is an independently run charity and does not receive revenue government funding and it is for this reason that charges are made for its exhibitions. It opens daily between 10am and 6pm, and until 10pm on a Friday. It has several excellent shops and restaurants within its grounds.

Burlington Arcade

Burlington Arcade, adjacent to the Royal Academy, was Britain's very first shopping Arcade. It opened in 1819 to great acclaim and is recognized as an historic and architectural masterpiece. The longest covered shopping street in England (a little under 60 m (196 ft)) and possibly the most beautiful, this oasis of calm is one of London's hidden treasures packed with luxurious accessories renowned throughout the world for their individuality and craftsmanship. Being so exclusive it is not surprising that it became the target of thieves in 1964. A jewellery heist took place when a Jaguar Mark X sports car sped through the arcade, six masked men jumped out from the car and having smashed the windows of the Goldsmiths and Silversmiths Association shop got away with jewellery worth about £35,000.

Beadles: Since 1819, the Arcade has been protected by the Beadles, liveried guards wearing traditional frock coats and braided top hats. Originally recruited by Lord Cavendish (later the Earl of Burlington) from his family regiment the 10th Hussars, they enforced his stipulated code of behavior in the Arcade. There was to be no whistling, singing, playing of musical instruments, running, carrying of large parcels or opening of umbrellas and no babies' prams. Today, these rules in the main still apply and the Beadles continue to patrol the Arcade and uphold these regulations with the full power to eject any visitor daring to contravene them.

MAYFAIR WALK AND AFTERNOON TEA

This walk takes you around Mayfair, one of London's most exclusive and prestigious areas, renowned throughout the globe for its wealth and beauty. It is in this small district that many of the gentlemen who frequented the shops and clubs around St James's, might have lived and it remains as one of London's prime addresses today.

Its name is derived from a fair held on 1st May each year from around the mid-17th century. Rowdy, and lasting about fourteen days, it ceased about a century later but its name attached itself to the area. As in nearby St James's, house building began here following the Great Fire of London 1666 when many sought housing away from the City of London in the east. Within one hundred years practically the entire area had been developed for residential purposes. From the start it was designed to attract the rich and was of great appeal with its wide straight avenues, graceful squares, several noblemen's palaces, mews

lined with stables and coach houses and shops servicing the wealthy.

Remarkably, Mayfair has retained much of its character despite suffering from WWII bombing and it still has the feel of real luxury and affluence. Its shopping streets are filled with designer shops, jewellers as well as art galleries and auction houses and there are many top-end hotels located here, especially around Park Lane and Grosvenor Square. It is therefore an area frequented by the rich and famous as well as art lovers and tourists!

Mayfair Tour: *Exit Burlington House, turn right (westwards) along Piccadilly and turn right when you reach Berkeley Street (4th turning). Walk to the end of the street towards Berkeley Square.*

1. Berkeley Square is one of Mayfair's most delightful oases. Walk into the gardens and enjoy this welcome green and leafy space dominated by a group of massive London plane trees, several well over 200 years old.

The square is also famous for Vera Lynn's romantic wartime song, 'A Nightingale Sang in Berkeley Square', although there is little evidence of those birds living in the vicinity now!

When the square was first constructed it was surrounded by residences lived in largely by the aristocracy. Sadly, wartime damage resulted in re-building of the south and east sides which are now large office blocks. However, the very beautiful terrace of Georgian housing on its west side still displays its wonderful 18th century features and character. Number 44 in particular, the work of William Kent, is much acclaimed. Upstairs the house is home to the Clermont Club, a well-known casino and gambling club, whilst the downstairs cellar, has been occupied by the nightclub Annabel's, frequented by celebrities and royals since it was first opened fifty years ago.

Leave the gardens through the north gate and turn left walking along Mount Street. At the junction with Carlos Place turn right by the Connaught Hotel and continue along the road until you reach Grosvenor Square.

2. Grosvenor Square. Home to the US Embassy since 1938, and full of statues and memorials with American associations, the square is only a stone's throw from the hustle and bustle of Oxford Street. Here you will see John Adams's house, statues of General Eisenhower, (whose military Headquarters were based at No 20 during WWII), Ronald Reagan and Franklin D Roosevelt, and the Memorial to the Eagle Squadron and the September 11 Memorial Garden. The Embassy is impossible to miss as it dominates the west side of the square and sports a giant gilded aluminium bald eagle on its roof! This however, is due to change in the near future when the Embassy moves to a new home south of the river and its building will no doubt be re-invented. Nonetheless, its presence here for the best part of eighty years will not be forgotten nor will the American association with the square.

Exit the square at the south-east corner crossing the road into Grosvenor Street. Turn right at Davies Street and when you reach Berkeley Square turn left until you arrive at Bruton Street with a luxury car showroom on the right hand side. As you walk along the street stop at the wall plaque about 20 m (65 ft) down on the right, and opposite the shops.

3. 17 Bruton Street. This address no longer exists but it was in a house on this site that HM The Queen was born on 21 April 1926 in the home of her maternal grandfather, the Earl of Strathmore. The princess was not born in a royal palace as her father was only second in line to be king at the time of her birth.

Unlike her great great grandmother, Queen Victoria, who was born at Kensington Palace, our present queen spent her early years in London, Richmond, Windsor and the country homes of her grandparents, and only moved into Buckingham Palace on her accession to the throne.

Across the road are the premises of 'Hartnell' – Couturier and official dressmaker to HM The Queen. Sir Norman Hartnell (1901–1979) established his business here in 1923 receiving his Royal Warrant in 1940 and a Knighthood in 1977. He was responsible for producing both the Queen's wedding and coronation gowns, which were two of his most famous commissions. A celebrated fashion designer who combined elegance with luxury and splendour, his label, the House of Hartnell, was sought after by movie stars, royalty and socialites everywhere.

Cast your eyes a few meters along the street to your right and you will see the names of a number of other noted fashion designers: Stella McCartney, Matthew Williamson, Brioni – a clear indication of the style, variety and exclusivity of shopping in this part of Mayfair. Walk down to the junction with New Bond Street where you will find designer shops in every direction.

4. Bond Street. With top fashion houses, perfumeries, jewellers, this is a seriously expensive street to shop! Home to Tiffany's, Graff, Mulberry, Cartier, Jimmy Choo and Alexander McQueen, Bond Street is very definitely high-end luxury shopping yet also caters for art lovers at the Halcyon Galleries and The Fine Art Society. Both Sotheby's and Bonham's auction houses are based here and

allow the public entrance to their viewings and sales.

'Bond Street' in reality does not exist as the street is divided into two: Old Bond Street and New Bond Street. The older part built in 1680 stretches south to Piccadilly whilst New Bond Street dating from

1730 goes north towards Oxford Street. Explore the area and you will find interesting side streets filled with contemporary and modern art galleries (as in Cork Street), or small independent boutiques, cafes and designer shops (South Molton Street), as well as courtyards, alleyways and even a museum, Handel House.

Turn right into New Bond Street and walk towards the pedestrianised section.

5. Allies Bench. Here you find a bench containing two very well known figures, Franklin D Roosevelt and Winston Churchill. These bronze models, the work of Lawrence Holofcener, appear to be having a conversation and look remarkably realistic. There is just enough space to nestle in between them and get your photograph taken chatting to the two grand old statesmen.

6. Brown's Hotel. To complete your afternoon trip around Mayfair why not sample a wonderful quintessential British afternoon tea in one of the district's oldest and loveliest hotels? Turn right into Grafton Street, then first left into Albemarle Street. A short walk brings you to Brown's Hotel, characterised by its exterior mosaics and grand entranceway. Established here in 1837, the year Queen Victoria came to the throne, it was set up by James Brown, valet to the poet, Lord Byron. He and his wife Sarah opened the hotel for 'genteel' folk, to cater for those who were in town 'for the season' (historically when the aristocratic families living in the country came to London to socialize, attends balls, the opera, charity events, dinner parties and for the young ladies, to find a suitable husband!).

The hotel became a great success and its reputation grew quickly. It was in this hotel that Teddy Roosevelt stayed before his wedding to Edith Carow in 1886. He walked from here to the Church in nearby Hanover Square. His distant relation, Franklin D Roosevelt, also stayed here in 1905, on honeymoon with his wife Eleanor. The author Rudyard Kipling was a guest whilst writing his famous novel, *The Jungle Book* and Brown's was the basis for Agatha Christie's book, At *Bertram's Hotel*. In 1876 the hotel was where Sir Alexander Graham Bell made the very first successful telephone call.

Brown's today is still one of Mayfair's most sophisticated and elegant hotels. Part of the Rocco Forte Collection it has the air of exclusive refinement and is the perfect spot to sample afternoon tea.

Afternoon Tea became a popular habit for women in the early 19th century. It was championed by Anna, the 7th Duchess of Bedford, a close friend of Queen Victoria, who is claimed to have experienced a 'sinking feeling' late afternoon. At this time the norm was to eat two meals a day; breakfast in the morning and an evening meal at around 8pm, so it was not surprising that the Duchess was feeling somewhat hungry by the afternoon. Her answer to her 'problem' was to take a pot of tea and a snack (bread and butter and a piece of cake) in the middle of the afternoon. Within very little time this had become common practice and the snack had become tiny sandwiches. Initially, food would be eaten in one's private boudoir but in time afternoon tea was provided in the Drawing Room of the house by London's social hostesses for their friends. Later in the 1880s afternoon tea became a tradition and aristocratic women and fashionable ladies would dress up for the occasion, tea being served between 4pm–5pm.

Afternoon tea nowadays is still a most civilised affair; tea from India or Ceylon poured into delicate china cups, petite sandwiches, pastries, cakes and maybe scones, jam and clotted cream. To make the meal even more special you may want to add a glass of champagne. Costs vary but expect to pay anything between £30 and £60, depending on where you decide to eat and what you choose to drink.

Brown's offers several types of afternoon tea ranging from about £45–£60. Sample menus can be seen on the hotel website: www.roccofortehotels.com

PICTURE CAPTIONS

1 - Liberty Department Store

2 - Hamley's Toy Store

3 - Floris

4 - Berry Bros and Rudd Wine Merchants

5 - Berry Bros and Rudd, Royal Warrant

6 - Fortnum & Mason Façade

7 - Brown's Hotel

8 - Bond Street

9 - "Allies" bench. Sculptor: Lawrence Holofcener

DAY 6

EXPLORING THE CITY OF LONDON

SECTION ONE

THE CITY — OLD AND NEW

THE CITY OF LONDON AND THE SQUARE MILE

The 'Square Mile' of London, is the original City of London, an area that dates back at least 2000 years. It was here that the Romans first crossed the River Thames and built the city of 'Londinium' which was to become a very significant trading post of their Empire for nearly 400 years. Not only did they transform the small settlement into a thriving city but they built magnificent buildings too. Not much is left of the Roman city now, but archaeological excavations have discovered the remains of a basilica, Governor's Palace, amphitheater, public baths, forum and even a fort. Since the Romans landed here in AD43, the city has been the focus of commerce and a successful port, although the latter declined in the later years of the 20th century. Today, one of the world's major financial districts along with New York and Tokyo, it is also a most important hub for world insurance, banking and financial services.

The whole area was severely damaged by fire on two occasions: in **1666**, at the time of the **Great Fire of London** when four fifths of the city's buildings were destroyed, and again during the war-time **Blitz in 1940-41**. The River Thames was a very easy target for bombers and the docks and buildings close to the river were regularly hit and suffered enormous damage and destruction. As a consequence you will find that the City is now a real mixture of old and new. Despite much fresh and innovative building in the post-war years much of the City's original piecemeal street pattern, its little alleyways and courtyards, still persist and it is not unusual to find a city church sandwiched between towering office blocks!

The City of London Corporation is responsible for the administration of the Square Mile and is lead by a Lord Mayor chosen by the Liverymen and Aldermen of the City of London (see sections on the Guildhall and Mansion House below), and is a position that dates back to the 12th century. Like many things in the City of London the role is full of tradition and pomp and circumstance, yet continues to be of the utmost importance today. It is the Lord Mayor acting as an ambassador, who represents London's and the UK financial and business interests as he travels the world and entertains foreign dignitaries, gives talks and addresses and is the major spokesman for the local authority.

The Guildhall is the administrative centre of the City of London Corporation whilst the Mayor's official home and office is at the Mansion House. **Day 6** begins at one of the city's oldest and most impressive buildings, St Paul's Cathedral.

St Paul's Cathedral and Churchyard

St Paul's Cathedral is undoubtedly a baroque masterpiece and was the first Protestant cathedral to be built after the Reformation of the 1530–40s. The present building is the fifth church on the site and the work of Sir Christopher Wren and his excellent team of hand-picked craftsmen.

Often referred to as the 'Nation's Church' the cathedral is largely used for services of Thanksgiving and Memorials although it has also been the location of two royal marriages (Arthur Tudor to Katherine of Aragon in 1501 and HRH Prince Charles to Lady Diana Spencer in 1981). In recent times it was the venue for the funeral ceremony of Baroness Thatcher, ex Conservative Prime Minister of the UK. A little over fifty years ago Sir Winston Churchill's coffin was brought here for his funeral service after a journey along the River Thames. During the 1800s funerals of great leaders such as Admiral Nelson and the Duke of Wellington were held in the cathedral before their burials in the cavernous crypt. Both the present monarch, Queen Elizabeth II and Queen Victoria have celebrated

Jubilee services here; so frail was Queen Victoria at her Diamond Jubilee in 1897, that the service had to be conducted outside the cathedral with the Queen sitting in the royal carriage with the congregation around her. (A painting depicting this scene can be seen in the Guildhall Art Gallery close by).

During the London Olympic Games in 2012 St Paul's Cathedral's bells rang out, the Olympic Torch Relay came to its steps, and a special summer service celebrating the Paralympic Games took place at the cathedral.

Whatever your interests, a visit to St Paul's should be at the top of your 'to-do' list of London, on account of its architecture, beauty and its colossal and quite wonderful dome, second only in size to St Peter's in Rome.

Inside St Paul's

The first thing one notices on entering the Cathedral is how light and spacious it feels. Wren had wanted light to stream through the building so when it was built all the windows were clear glass. He also intended to keep the interior uncluttered. Over time however, monuments and memorials were added mainly along the aisles and beneath the Dome, but there are still far fewer here than in

Westminster Abbey.

As you walk through the nave you may be surprised to see a memorial (sarcophagus) of the Duke of Wellington surmounted by his horse, Copenhagen. Certainly, a source of great controversy at the time it was made, it took almost fifty years following the Duke's death before the church authorities would allow it to be placed in the Cathedral!

Despite its plain beginnings, there has been much greater color and adornment within the cathedral since Victorian times. Queen Victoria declared that she found the place to be 'dull, dreary and undevotional', so towards the end of her reign brightly colored mosaics were added to the Nave and Choir sections. Again, after WWII, when the American Chapel was installed behind the High Altar, stained glass windows were added providing further color to the east end of the church.

Considered by many to be Wren's magnus opus, the Dome is not entirely how it appears! To get a real understanding of it, sit in one of the pews beneath the structure and look up. What you may not realize is that the Dome you are peering into is actually one of two, an inner and outer dome, with a brick cone between them. Wren built this complex structure in order to accommodate the massive outer Dome, an unusual feature and the first of its kind in the country. Not only very high, the Dome and lantern above weigh over 700 tons and that weight is carried by the eight piers placed beneath it. Beautiful Italian mosaics, gifts of the Livery companies, embellish the area between the piers whilst in contrast James Thornhill's superb grisaille paintings of the Life of St Paul, decorate the interior of the Dome above.

Half-way up the Dome you will see railings which surround the Whispering Gallery, a place where because of its acoustics, whispers on one of side can be heard perfectly by anyone standing opposite! If you are good with heights then this is well worth a visit. You can also climb a further 271 steps up to the Golden Gallery outside from where you will obtain excellent views of the city's buildings and skyline.

On the floor beneath the Dome look out for the latin inscription, 'Lector, si monumentum requiris, circumspice' (Reader, if you seek his monument, look around you) – the Cathedral's memorial to the work of its architect, Sir Christopher Wren.

Wren was assisted in his work by a team of very talented craftsmen; men like James Thornhill (Hogarth's father-in-law), Jean Tijou, master iron-worker, Grinling Gibbons, celebrated wood-carver, and brothers Edward and Thomas Strong, master masons. Their work is especially apparent in the carving of the pews, organ casing, iron gates, and stone work within the nave and chancel areas, and the 17th century organ is still in use today.

High Altar and American Chapel

Walk along the south quire aisle on the right hand side of the Cathedral until you reach the beautiful iron Tijou Gates on your left and mount the few steps towards the high altar. Re-built in the post-war restoration of St Paul's the high altar is made of marble and carved and gilded oak. The glorious canopy above is based on a drawing of Christopher Wren that was not implemented in his life and is surmounted by Christ in Majesty. Beneath the canopy is a fine memorial to soldiers from the Commonwealth and Empire who lost their lives fighting in the 1939–1945 World War.

Now pass into the American Chapel in the apse at the east end of the building. It is dedicated to the 28,000 Americans stationed in the country who died in WWII and was erected by the British people as a gesture of gratitude for their support. Opened in 1958 the Chapel's brightly colored windows contain the emblems of each of the fifty US states. Other US connections are featured here too such as the date when the first US colony was founded at Jamestown in 1607. If you look carefully you will find Eisenhower's head carved in wood at the end of the pew benches as he was the President of America when the idea of the chapel was conceived. More subtle and disguised amid the wood carving is a rocket, commemorating the role of the US in space exploration.

The Crypt

Here you will find Wren's tomb placed under a plain marble slab, so unassuming that it would be easy to pass it by! As no memorial could exceed that of the Cathedral itself, the grave is probably most fitting.

Surrounding the tomb are memorials and graves of famous artists and musicians: Sir Joshua Reynolds, Anthony Van Dyck, Hubert Parry, J E Millais, John Singer Sargent, George Frampton.

Here too is the Chapel of the Order of the British Empire which is the most junior and most populous order of chivalry in the British honors system. Established by King George V in 1917 initially to honor those who had served in many non-combatant capacities in the 1914–18 World War, the honor nowadays is conferred on the civil population too. Many actors, sportsmen and women, fashion designers, media personnel and singers have received honors in the past century given by the Queen on the advice of her government.

Now with the Chapel behind you walk through the pews towards the far railings and you will reach two tombs of men responsible for defeating Napoleon in the early 19th century. The first is that of the Duke of Wellington, a plain yet impressive tomb in Cornish granite. When Wellington died in 1851 the streets were lined with thousands of mourners and it is said that over 8000 people attended his service within the Cathedral! As a military leader he was very popular with his men and celebrated for never having lost a battle. After leaving the military he became involved in politics and went on to become Prime Minister and Constable of the Tower of London where he was lauded for his public service. His name is forever associated with Wellington boots and the dish 'Beef Wellington' and remembered for phrases such as, 'The Battle of Waterloo was won on the playing fields of Eton'.

The tomb of Horatio, Admiral Lord Nelson is also close by, actually sited immediately beneath the Dome. Having been hit by a French sniper he died on his ship, the Victory, in 1805 at the Battle of Trafalgar, but in the knowledge that Napoleon had been defeated. Nelson's body, it is said, was placed in a barrel full of alcohol and returned to England and after a state funeral within the cathedral, was later buried here. The black marble sarcophagus you see was one that Cardinal Wolsey (Lord Chancellor to Henry VIII) had made for himself in the 1500s, but after his fall from favour was never used. Wolsey's cardinal's hat was subsequently replaced by Nelson's viscount coronet.

Walking around the Crypt is like taking a tour of British history with memorials and plaques commemorating military and naval officers, conflicts and wars over the last 200-300 years, including one commemorating the 'Lady with the Lamp', Florence Nightingale.

When you leave the Crypt you will find refreshments and toilet facilities in the lobby area as well as a remarkably well-stocked shop. There is a small café providing light refreshments and a Cathedral restaurant which offers fine dining and is open for lunch and afternoon tea. Exit from the crypt up the flight of stairs and then turn right towards the churchyard.

Churchyard

Walk through this quiet enclosed area and stop for a moment by the statue of preacher, John Wesley, who founded the Methodist church, and lived and worked in the neighbourhood. In the distance you can see a tall column, St Paul's Cross.

The monument dates to the early 1900s, but replaces a much earlier cross that had stood close by here between the 9th and 17th centuries, and was the place people came to for news. Before newspapers existed and when the majority of the population were illiterate, this spot was **the** news centre of London, the 'Times' newspaper of its day! Religious proclamations, papal bulls and edicts, sermons, national addresses, royal births, deaths and marriages, denunciations of traitors, all the main affairs of state were announced from the Cross.

In the late 15th century it had become a very grand, spacious, open-air timber pulpit, with a lead roof, reached by a flight of stone steps, but was later destroyed when the Puritans ruled the country in the mid 1600s and it was never re-built.

Exit the churchyard at the east end gate, cross Cheapside and walk down the street. Turn left at King Street. At the junction, cross Gresham Street and walk directly towards the Guildhall.

THE GUILDHALL, GUILDHALL YARD AND ART GALLERY

The Guildhall is the largest secular stone City building to have survived both the Great Fire of London 1666 and the heavy bombing of WWII. It is here that the City of London Corporation is located and administers the Square Mile, a role it has carried out for over 800 years! Nowadays, it is one of 33 London local authorities and is by far the richest despite being the smallest!

Based in Guildhall Yard the 14th century building is flanked on both sides by additions from the 20th century, the Court of Aldermen and Guildhall Library to the west and the Guildhall Art Gallery to the east, and also shares the site with St Lawrence Jewry church. The church is now the official church of the City of London, and used on ceremonial occasions. Like many of the City churches it offers a wonderful programme of lunch-time recitals and concerts, many of which are free.

Black tiles on the floor of the yard denote the extent of the Roman amphitheater, discovered in the 1980s when the foundations of the Art Gallery were begun, and now a protected monument. If you enter the Art Gallery be sure to visit the reconstruction of the amphitheater down in the basement which gives some insight into its scope. Tours explaining the remains and describing the gladiatorial activities that would have occurred here 2000 years ago are offered on Fridays.

Upstairs, the Art Gallery displays both permanent and temporary exhibits, many featuring or related to London, as well as works by the Pre-Raphaelite artists such as Dante Gabriel Rossetti and John Everett Millais. Of particular note is 'The Defeat of the Floating Batteries at Gibraltar', an enormous work of American painter John Singleton Copley that dominates the largest gallery.

A visit to the Guildhall is free, the building opens daily and is a real delight to visit (but do check first on website as it sometimes closes at short notice due to public events). It is here that the monthly meeting of the Court of Common Council (the City of London's elected Assembly) takes place and where State Banquets, Ceremonies and other major public engagements and entertainments are held.

On entering the Great Hall look up to view the lofty oak-panelled roof, the fifth in situ since the Guildhall was first constructed in the 15th century, and then lower your gaze to see the banners of the twelve Great Livery Companies hanging over a decorative frieze. The Hall is vast, said to be one of the largest civic halls in England, and is lined either side with monuments of great British heroes such as Nelson, Wellington and Winston Churchill. Many statesmen have stood in the Hall over the centuries some to receive honors such as the Freedom of the City, others to address the Lord Mayor and Common Council. During the 16th century the Hall was also the setting for state trials, most notably that of the nine day queen, Lady Jane Grey, and of Archbishop Cranmer. Each September, on Michaelmas Day, the Hall is used to elect a new Lord Mayor and in November it becomes the venue of the 'Silent Ceremony' when the new Lord Mayor is installed in his office.

Turn round to face the Minstrels' Gallery above the main entrance door to see two giant statues: Gog and Magog. These are mythical representations of a conflict between Britons and Trojan invaders after which 'New Troy' (subsequently London), was established. The statues, long associated with the City of London, often appear alongside the many colorful floats at the Lord Mayor's Show in November.

Beneath the Great Hall is probably one of the City's greatest hidden treasures: a medieval undercroft divided into two crypts. The crypts are not always accessible to the public but if they are open on the day you visit do have a quick peek. The western side is believed to even pre-date the Great Hall above. It disappeared for about 300 years and was only re-discovered when major restoration was undertaken in the building in the 1970s.

Now re-trace your steps to Cheapside, and turn right. Cross the road and enter.

One New Change

Apart from providing a good range of shops the centre is known for its fabulous roof-top bar and restaurant from where you enjoy spectacular views of the River Thames and the London skyline. A bonus is the glass elevator ride up to the roof which has been designed in such a way as to frame the dome of the cathedral showing us its magnificent structure.

This shopping mall, designed by top architect Jean Nouvel, has not only instilled new life into the area, but has actually returned Cheapside to its former role of a major shopping street. The word 'chepe' from the Anglo-Saxon means 'market', and indeed much trade took place here throughout the centuries. Until the twelfth century Cheapside functioned as one of London's major markets; by the 1500s it was well established as a centre of commerce and industry. Today, if you walk around the district you will still see local streets named Bread, Honey and Milk Street, reflecting their former usage. As a major link between the historic City of London, the law courts and Parliament in Westminster it has always functioned as a significant thoroughfare and remains important to this day.

Roof top

Take the elevator up to the roof, and then turn left on to the terrace. If you arrive here at the end of the working day you will it full of 'suits', lawyers, bankers, management consultants, office staff and hedge fund managers who work in the City, relaxing either at the bar or in the restaurant. It is extremely popular for its location, cocktail bar and dining. It is an exciting place to be at sunset as you have an excellent view of the River Thames and the South Bank, the City skyline, as well as St Paul's Cathedral.

LONDON'S OPEN SPACES, WATERWAYS AND MARKETS

With eight Royal Parks (four in central London), the newly formed Queen Elizabeth Olympic Park, and green spaces like London Fields and Victoria Park in east London, Battersea and Greenwich Parks in the south and Alexandra Palace park in the north, you will always be able to find somewhere to enjoy life in the open air during your stay. Added to these are the many churchyards spaces, piazzas, rivers, canals, lakes and ponds where you can chill out, stroll alongside the water, or have a picnic.

Regent's Park, on the edge of the West End is home to London Zoo which is the world's oldest scientific zoo, and where you can easily devote an entire day! The park has plenty of outdoor activities: two boating lakes, (one especially for children), children's playgrounds, its own Open-Air Theater, pitches for football, as well as the beautiful Queen Mary rose gardens. Landscaped by John Nash

in the early 19th Century for the Prince Regent he also designed the striking stucco 'Nash Terraces' that surround the park.

The **Queen Elizabeth Olympic Park** (QEOP) is a significant legacy of the London 2012 Olympic and Paralympic games. Based to the east of London in Stratford (not to be confused with Shakespeare's birthplace, Stratford-upon-Avon in Warwickshire), the park is also home to the Olympic Stadium, Aquatic Centre, Lee Valley Velopark, Lee Valley Hockey and Tennis Centre, the Copper Box Arena, East Village, Here East and the largest sculpture in the UK, the ArcelorMittal Orbit. In addition it has several miles of waterways, woods, parkland and themed walking trails. Take a guided tour or a boat trip to discover about the 2012 games, try out the Velopark or go for a swim in the Olympic sized pools within the Aquatic Centre designed by Iraqi-British architect, Dame Zaha Hadid. The park also contains an area of climbing walls and some excellent children play spaces. The Olympic Stadium was recently a 2015 Rugby World

Cup venue and is shortly due to become home to West Ham United Football Club and to double up as the National Competition Centre for UK Athletics.

The park is remarkably accessible, reached by using the Jubilee line, London Overground, and national rail. There is even an 8 minute, express train service linking Stratford with King's Cross, but if you prefer catch a bus into the West End and the City.

London has always been blessed with rivers some of which were renowned in former times for their healing qualities! Many rivers like the Walbrook, Westbourne and Fleet are now lost or pass beneath London's streets into the river Thames, but since the early 19th century the **Regent's Canal** has run from the west of London to Limehouse in the east by the Thames. Nowadays, it is possible to walk on towpaths beside the canal and acquaint yourself with the different neighbourhoods through which the water flows. Close to Paddington you find the most pretty of enclaves, **Little Venice**. Here the Grand Union Canal (from the north) joins the Regent's Canal and there is a small basin characterized by its colorful narrow boats, barges and even the occasional wherry. At the beginning of May a boating cavalcade is held in the basin when the whole area is bedecked with bunting, food stalls appear and there is generally a feeling of carnival about the place. With beautiful (and expensive) housing all about, atmospheric Victorian pubs as well as graceful weeping willow trees, clematis and climbing roses, Little Venice is quite unique in London and an ideal place to visit at any time of the year.

Transport: Warwick Avenue (Bakerloo line), Paddington (Bakerloo, Hammersmith and City, Circle and District lines).

Central London is naturally dominated by the River Thames where you find many sightseeing boat tours, London Duck tours (a river and road experience), and high- speed rib tours! If you fancy a boat trip on the river look at www.tfl.gov.uk for details about the many river services on offer.

You might even like to try your hand at rowing or perhaps 'exercise' your legs on a pedalo. Many of London's parks have boating lakes where you can hire a boat for 30-60 minutes at a time. There are generally good paths beside the lakes and taking time out here may be a super respite from the hustle and bustle of shopping in Oxford Street or after a bout of sightseeing.

Another suggestion is to visit to one of the many and varied markets that exist in the city. If food is what interests you most then possibly a visit to **Smithfield**, London's wholesale meat market, or **Billingsgate Fish Market**, close by Canary Wharf, is something to include in your itinerary. Certainly, **Borough Market** (Day 4) should not be missed on account of its marvelous food displays, and for its specialist foods, delicacies, wine and beer. This is the place to go for organic produce, and the greatest selection of high quality food. Everywhere you turn you find people sampling morsels of cheese, ham, salamis, and waiting at the very busy stalls selling lunchtime snacks.

Petticoat Lane in the East End, is a fairly general market today selling clothing, household goods, bags, jewellery, as well as bric-a-brac! In contrast, trendy **Camden Market** in north London is where you can find alternative fashion, African and Asian art, vintage clothing, leatherware, antiques, rugs, clothing and second-hand books. It sprawls by and around the Regent's Canal and has several thriving food courts offering enticing fare from nearly every continent in the world.

On a Sunday morning go east to **Columbia Road Market** which specializes in plants and flowers. When the market closes around lunchtime you can then spend time browsing in some of the interesting shops along the street or pop into a local pub for a bite to eat!

London has a great selection of antique markets too, each of which opens on different days of the week: Visit **Camden Passage** (by Angel, Islington) on Wednesday and Saturday, **Old Spitalfields Market** on Thursday, **Bermondsey Square** on Friday, **Portobello Road** on Saturday. **Alfies Antique Market**, in Marylebone (Church Street) and **Grays** by Bond Street Station are open most weekdays and are indoor markets.

SECTION TWO

WALKING TOUR OF THE CITY

1. Bank Junction – Via Decumana

An exceptionally busy spot with five roads radiating from its centre it has always been an important junction and was the heart of Roman London two thousand years ago! At that time, the **Via Decumana,** today's Poultry, was the major street through the Roman settlement.

2. Bank of England

Stand on the island facing the Royal Exchange and on your left you will see a building of fortress-like proportions, the Bank of England. Sitting on a deceptively large island site the Bank if made of up 3 storeys below ground plus 7 above. The upper section was added in the 1920-30s, designed by Sir Herbert Baker, who is best known for his monumental imperial buildings within the Commonwealth countries.

Most of Sir John Soane's original 18th century single storey grand classical building was demolished at this time yet his perimeter windowless walls were retained and are what gives the structure a feeling of force.

The Bank has had the nickname, 'The Old Lady of Threadneedle Street' since 1797 when a cartoon by satirist, James Gilray was published. Officially entitled 'Political Ravishment or The Old Lady of Threadneedle Street in danger', it showed the Prime Minister, William Pitt the Younger, pretending to court the Bank, (represented by an older lady wearing a dress of £1 notes and sitting on a chest of gold). Look above the main Threadneedle Street doorway and you will see the lady, still obvious in the pediment.

The Bank, was founded in 1694 by William Paterson, a Scotsman and prominent City banker, largely to help fund and raise capital for war against the French. Today, the Bank has many functions: as the Government's Bank, printer of banknotes, (having had a monopoly for this since 1844), guardian of currency. It holds the nations' gold and foreign exchange currency reserves and since, 1997, sets interest rates independent of the Treasury. It claims to be the largest reserve in the world along with Fort Knox and NY Federal Reserve Bank.

In 2013 a new Governor of the Bank of England was appointed, a Canadian, Mark Carney. Controversy ensued both in relation to his nationality and his salary, said to be the highest ever paid! The importance of the role cannot be understated and it is interesting to note that the former governor, on leaving office was awarded the honor of Knight Companion of the Order of the Garter, the oldest and most important British order of chivalry.

If you are visiting on a weekday try to pop into the Bank's excellent museum which is free and open from 10am-5pm. It contains a great variety of artefacts relevant to the Bank's history as well as permanent displays explaining the Bank's role in today's economy and how it works to protect the financial system from economic shocks. Children will enjoy attempting to pick up a gold bar whilst fans of Kenneth Grahame, author of 'The Wind in the Willows', will be keen to learn more about his years of employment as Secretary to the Bank.

3. Mansion House

This imposing stone building with its grand staircase and columns is the Mansion House, official home to the Lord Mayor, whilst he/she carries out duties in the year of office. Here, visiting dignitaries, Heads of State, senior politicians and businessmen are entertained in one of the many sumptuous rooms. Designed in the mid-18th century in the Palladian style by George Dance the Elder, the building is a delight of Georgian architecture and decoration. Famed for its lavish

Egyptian Hall, which despite its name is not Egyptian in decoration but rather more based on Roman buildings in Egypt, as well as its priceless 17th century Dutch and Flemish art collection, Mansion House opens for a guided tour every Tuesday afternoon as well as on the yearly Open House weekend in September.

Because the Lord Mayor is the Chief Magistrate of the City of London, there are cells beneath the building (into which Emmeline Pankhurst, the Suffragette women's rights campaigner and leader was incarcerated in the early 20th century), as well as a Court Room, though neither is in use today.

Since 2000, The Lord Mayor of the City of London is one of three London Mayors. He himself is elected for a one-year term on Michaelmas Day in September. His counterpart, the Lord Mayor of Westminster, is elected by residents also for one year, whilst the Mayor of London, is voted in by London's registered electorate for a four year term and has jurisdiction over the whole of Greater London.

The very first Lord Mayor appointed in 1189 was Henry Fitzailwyn and 25 years later the office and status of the Mayor and Corporation was further embedded when King John signed the Magna Carta, a document giving rights and liberties to the City fathers. (There is a gallery devoted to the Magna Carta within the Guildhall Art Gallery). It is interesting to note that the Corporation of London actually pre-dated the British Parliament as the first democratic metropolitan authority and remains the guardian of the interests of the City, managing its planning, buildings, open spaces, economy, arts facilities, and a host of other areas similarly covered by other London boroughs.

4. Alleyways and Coffee Houses – Off Cornhill going east

The City of London has a somewhat chaotic street pattern developed over many centuries and was never a planned urban area. Before the Great Fire of London in 1666 its buildings were made from wood and many of the houses overhung the narrow streets below. Even when the fire destroyed nearly all of the City's buildings they were re-built in a similar fashion, despite plans having been proposed for a new grid-like street plan to be adopted. The city thus retained its original atmosphere and the narrow streets and alleyways were reconstructed much as they had always been.

The first Coffee House in London was established in St Michael's Alley, where in 1652, a merchant and trader in Turkish goods, Daniel Edwards, set up his servant, Pasqua Rosee in business, selling coffee at a penny a cup. Many other coffee houses appeared nearby and each associated with different area of interest, laying the foundations for many of the City's commodity markets. It was in these establishments that merchants met establishing contacts and doing business not too dissimilar to many working people today! At the time each

coffee house appealed to different groups of people. A number were frequented by Americans like the New York Coffee House, which from 1730 was the centre of intelligence for all connected with the American trade, the Pennsylvania, that catered for shipping interests, the Jerusalem, Virginia & Baltic. Others, including Lloyd's, became associated with marine insurance, and Garraway's, was frequented by stock jobbers during the South Sea Bubble in 1720.

5. Leadenhall Market

The current Leadenhall Market (located between Leadenhall and Lime Streets) was purpose built as a covered market in the late 1800s when wrought iron and glass were introduced. Lined with small shops, painted brightly and with a wonderful roof the market still attracts thousands of visitors, office workers and tourists. Lunch times are especially busy when a number of pop-up stalls appear offering cuisine from every part of the globe, and always at very reasonable prices.

Recent archaeological excavations have discovered that the present market hall is built over a former market place

dating back nearly two thousand years. It was on this site in the 2nd century that the Romans built their Forum, (marketplace) and Basilica, (Law Courts). At that time it was the largest such site in the Roman Empire north of the Alps and spread over an area bigger than Trafalgar Square!

This part of Roman London is where business was carried out, deals formed and merchants traded their wares. Much has been unearthed over the years giving us an insight as to how the original Roman buildings were constructed and what they must have looked like. Mosaic pavements have been found as well as other artifacts from the Roman period, and you will find these rare and wonderful objects on display at the Museum of London by the Barbican.

Interestingly, the area was once again in use as a market for poulterers and cheesemongers in the 1300s, and continued in this role over the next century. When London was devastated by the Great Fire in 1666 the market buildings were badly damaged and had to be rebuilt. The market subsequently operated as a Beef Market, Herb Market and a Green Yard.

Fans of the Harry Potter books and films might well recognize the setting as the location of Diagon Alley in the movie, 'Harry Potter and the Philosopher's Stone'. It is here that Harry accompanied by Hagrid, comes shopping for an owl and a broomstick and after visiting Eeylops Owl Emporium buys a snowy owl, whom he names Hedwig.

6. City Architecture

Emerging from the market you will be surrounded by some really exciting contemporary architecture that characterizes the late 20th and 21st century City of London.

The first building you come across and surely one of the City's most iconic, if not most controversial buildings, is the high-tech **Lloyd's of London** designed by leading architect Richard Rogers. Now a Grade I listed building it has become accepted as part of the fabric of the city but when it was constructed in the 1980s was initially the brunt of much criticism and caused great debate.

Adjacent to Lloyd's is the **Willis Building** designed by architect Norman Foster with a 'stepped' design planned to look like a crustacean shell. From its curved glass exterior you gain some wonderful views of the Lloyd's building. It is 125 m (410 ft) tall with 26 storeys and when it opened in 2008 was one of the tallest buildings in the City.

The Leadenhall Building, right opposite has a very distinctive triangular shape which was created in order to protect the views of St Paul's Cathedral. Designed by Rogers Stirk Harbour and Partners it opened in 2014 and has become better known as 'The Cheesegrater'.

Just around the corner from this building is another structure which has become a true London landmark. Officially, **30 St Mary Axe** it is better known as the **The Gherkin.** Designed by Norman Foster and Arup engineers, it was built in 2003 with 40 floors, standing on the former site of the Baltic Exchange building, which had been severely damaged in1992 by a bomb explosion.

Since its completion, the building has won a number of prestigious awards for architecture. It has also featured in movies such as *Harry Potter and the Half Blood Prince*, Sharon Stone's *Basic Instinct 2,* Woody Allen's *Match Point* and the romantic comedy, *Mamma Mia*.

Also in the area is **Tower 42**, one of London's very first skyscrapers and the tallest building (183 m (600 ft)) present in the Square Mile for three decades, only surpassed by the **Heron Tower** in 2010. Built for the National Westminster Bank it was originally known as the Nat West Tower. Not surprisingly, as the first skyscraper to be constructed in a somewhat conservative City of London, it was a contentious addition to the City's skyline, yet from its inception it was always a landmark. The Tower underwent total refurbishment in the 1990s and then sold to new owners who renamed it 'Tower 42' due to its 42 cantilevered floors.

Since changing hands the building is no longer solely used by bankers but is now shared by a variety of City companies ranging from hedge funds, corporate lawyers and solicitors, to securities and investment firms as well as a some overseas banks, demonstrating the many different faces of the financial City of London.

To get superb views of the city you might want to visit its rooftop bar or eat at Vertigo, Tower 42's renowned restaurant.

7. The Royal Exchange – Bank Junction

This is a building that since its foundation in 1566 has been the hub of the City of London's trade and commercial life. The present Victorian building is the third on the site, yet its purpose remains much the same – a place where traders, albeit very up-market ones, meet with consumers and a good deal of money passes hands!

When it was constructed in the 16th century the building not only provided a trading floor but also two further storeys above with small individual outlets leased to about a hundred shopkeepers. It was the first real indoor shopping mall in London and the country. Today, once again the Exchange is full of small luxury goods stores greatly suited for its clientele of bankers, lawyers and businessmen and women. There is even a bar/café in the original trading floor space, the ideal venue for a business meeting, so central to the nearby banking, insurance and financial offices.

From the start the Exchange had been associated with major City institutions, their employees buying and selling goods and insurances and negotiating deals within its walls. In the 16th century metal traders convened here, it became home to the Stock Exchange at the end of the 1600s, and towards the end of the 18th century Lloyd's of London took up premises in the building where it remained until the 1920s.

The constant relationship of the Royal Exchange with commerce is highlighted in sculptures on the pediment that stands above the porticoed entrance. Here you see Commerce (represented by a female statue) in the centre with City merchants on either side of her.

The importance of this building not only to commerce but to the City of London is further demonstrated by the fact that it is from the Royal Exchange's steps that the death of the monarch is announced and the accession of the new king or queen proclaimed.

8. St Lawrence Jewry Church – Guildhall Yard

This church located in Guildhall Yard was re-built by Sir Christopher Wren after the Great Fire of 1666, and is said to be one of his most expensive churches. It suffered extensive bomb damage during World War II and was later restored. Today it is the official church of the Lord Mayor of London and the City of London Corporation and services are held here daily as well as wonderful free lunchtime recitals on the piano and organ every Monday and Tuesday at 1pm. Both are to be recommended and it is all the more special to listen to music played on a piano once owned by the conductor Sir Thomas Beecham. Ornately decorated with gold leaf and grand chandeliers it is a very beautiful church and worth a visit.

Its name, St Lawrence Jewry, distinguishes it from other churches dedicated to St Lawrence in the City of London in earlier times. 'Jewry' was added to its name due to its proximity to the road where the Jewish population settled between 1066 and 1290 until they were expelled from the country by King Edward I.

9. St Mary Aldermanbury Church and Gardens – Love Lane

This garden is the site of another church, dating from the 12th century that was destroyed in 1666. Subsequently rebuilt by Christopher Wren, it was again badly damaged by the Blitz in 1940, leaving only the walls standing. In 1966 the church stones were transported by the residents of Fulton, Missouri, to their town in the USA and rebuilt in the grounds of Westminster College as a memorial to Winston Churchill who had made his Sinews of Peace, "Iron Curtain" speech in the Westminster College Gymnasium in 1946.

Following the removal of the stones the site of the church and churchyard was planted with bushes and trees in the shape of the original church.

The adjacent gardens, contain a monument surmounted with a bust of William Shakespeare. The monument is dedicated to two Elizabethan actors who lived in the parish and were buried in the churchyard: Henry Condell and John Heminges. Not only co-partners with and very close friends of William Shakespeare at the Globe Theater the men were important for producing the First Folio of Shakespeare's plays after his death. It was they who separated the plays into Histories, Tragedies and Comedies, which is how they have been referred to ever since.

10. Roman wall and fort – Noble Street

In around AD120 the Romans built a fort to the north-west of their main settlement of Londinium. It is believed that it was constructed as a barracks to house up to one thousand men accommodating all the troops stationed in the city at the time. It was over 200 m (650 ft) on each side and had rounded corners. Almost a square it covered nearly 12 acres, had 5 m (16.4 ft) high stone walls and these were strengthened by earth banks on the inside.

Roughly 80 or so years later a city wall was constructed around Londinium and the wall was constructed so that it joined the north-east and south-west corners of the fort. The ruins that you see here are the remains of a corner tower that was located at the south west side of the fort. This is the final stop of the walk but if you want to discover more about Roman London visit the Museum of London by the Barbican (see below).

SMITHFIELD

This is the boundary between the City of London and the London Borough of Islington. Its name, 'Smithfield', derives from 'Smooth Field' as it was once just that – a swamp on the edge of the City of London.

It has a great history of blood and death: The Romans buried their dead here and during Tudor times in the reigns of Mary Tudor and Queen Elizabeth I Protestants and Catholics alike, were burnt at the stake or executed here. 16th century witches and heretics were also subject to such activity and the area became synonymous with hanging, disemboweling and torture.

During the Plague of 1665, Smithfield was used as a mass burial pit, and the following year the area escaped the ravages of the Great Fire only thanks to the ditch that separated it from the City and a sudden change in the direction of the wind.

In addition the area was the site for Medieval tournaments, jousting, horse races, demonstrations and the wonderful boisterous Bartholomew Fair, an annual event which lasted from 1123–1855!

St Bartholomew's Fair, was originally held over 3 days every August. A public holiday for Londoners and attracting European cloth merchants, it was opened by the Lord Mayor by the cutting of a piece of cloth, (the origin of the custom of ribbon-cutting to open events or buildings). By the 1600s the fair had deteriorated into a much longer and riotous affair with sideshows, entertainers, bull and bear-baiting. Victorian disapproval led to its final demise in the 1850s and Londoners lost their oldest public holiday; Bank Holidays were not introduced until 1871.

Charles Dickens (1812–1870) in his book 'Oliver Twist' gives a wonderful description of Oliver crossing Smithfield on market day and alludes to the thick steam that arose from the stinking bodies of the cattle as well as the dirt and sludge all around the place. Two centuries earlier Ben Jonson (1572–1637) wrote the comedy of manners, 'Bartholomew Fair' (1614) describing the annual fair held at Smithfield, whilst Samuel Pepys recorded an account of his visit to the fair in 1668 in his famous diary.

In addition to the Fair, Smithfield has been home to a market since 975, and was awarded a market charter in the s. It occupies a ten acre site just within the City boundaries and was originally a live cattle market, at a time when slaughtering and leather tanning were tolerated only away from the City centre.

Since 1855 however Smithfield has been a 'dead meat' market, and a far less 'bloody' place! The market halls you see here date back to the 1860s, and were designed by Horace Jones, the man responsible for other city markets in Billingsgate and Leadenhall (as well as Tower Bridge). When it was built the market cost £2m to construct and was the largest in the world. It even had railway sidings in the basement, (now a car park) so that deliveries could be kept separate from the market traders above.

Renovations took place about 25 years ago when modern robotic equipment was introduced. It is still very much a hive of activity during the night attracting a wide range of buyers including top class chefs and restaurant owners from all over London. Most of the action is over by 9.30am, and everything closed by noon, but because of the nature of the business you will be able to get a drink at one of the local pubs very early in the morning!

St Bartholomew the Great:

A religious priory was established in Smithfield in 1123 by Rahere, a jester in Henry II's court, who had been sick on a pilgrimage to the Holy Land. On recovering he vowed to set up a priory and hospital on his return home to London. Although the Priory was dissolved in the 1530s, it then became a parish church, whilst the hospital was later re-founded by King Henry VIII and both are still in use almost 500 years later.

The church is famous for its wonderful preserved Norman architecture with its heavy columns, piers and round arches and Rahere's grand and elaborate tomb can be seen within. The artist, William Hogarth was baptised here in November 1697, and American, Benjamin Franklin, author, politician, statesman and inventor, worked on a printing press in the Lady Chapel in the 18th century.

4 Weddings and a Funeral, Shakespeare in Love, The End of the Affair, Amazing Grace, Elizabeth: The Golden Age, The Other Boleyn Girl, and Robin Hood, Prince of Thieves have all been filmed here. It has also appeared in a number of television programmes including *Madame Bovary, The Real Sherlock Holmes, Spooks, Edwin Drood, Richard II and The League of Gentlemen Christmas Special.*

St Bartholomew's Hospital (Barts) is now a leading teaching hospital and has become a centre for the treatment of cancer, cardiac conditions and fertility problems.

MUSEUM OF LONDON – THE BARBICAN

This is another of London's treasures, a brilliant museum devoted wholly to London, its history and social background. Perched on a roundabout right by the Barbican Arts Complex it is open daily from 10am–6pm with collections dating from prehistoric time right to the present day.

Although it underwent a major refurbishment in 2010 the museum still remains desperately short of space to display its many objects. At the time of writing (2015) plans have been announced for a move by 2021 from its Barbican site to nearby Smithfield Market's General Market Building. This would allow it to increase its gallery space and display more of its many unseen pieces.

Presently, the collections are exhibited on two levels and are wonderfully diverse. Where else could you see a Roman bikini, a pair of stylish Medieval shoes dating from the late 14th century, Oliver Cromwell's death mask (England's protector during the Civil War of the 17th century), a mosaic from a Roman London house, and the skull of an extinct auroch (wild ox) dating from 245,000–186,000 BC?

Downstairs on Level 2 the **Victorian Walk** recreates the shops, smells and atmosphere of 19th century London, transporting you back to the world of Dickens.

See also the magnificent and opulent Lord Mayor's State Coach used every November when it is driven through London at the Lord Mayor's Parade shortly after the newly appointed mayor takes up his position. It is the most beautifully crafted vehicle reflecting the importance of the role of Lord Mayor.

The World City: 1850s–today, is wonderfully nostalgic for anyone who visited or lived in the capital in the latter part of the 20th century, displaying the 1959 Vespa scooter which was so much a part of Swinging 60s London, Mary Quant and Biba clothing as well as fashion and jewellery of more modern designers such as Alexander McQueen and Tatty Devine.

A recent addition to the museum and something you may also recognize is the 2012 Cauldron, unveiled at the London Olympic Games opening ceremony.

The museum offers free gallery tours at 11am, midday, 3pm and 4pm, has good cloakroom facilities as well as two cafes and a surprisingly good shop with a vast range of books on (as you would expect) London and many interesting gifts.

Barbican Underground Station (*Circle and Metropolitan lines*) is two minutes walk from the Museum or you can catch a *Central line* train from nearby St Paul's Station.

PICTURE CAPTIONS

1 - St Paul's Cathedral Dome

2 - John Wesley statue

3 - St Michael's Alley, Jamaica Wine House

4 - Leadenhall Market

5 - City Architecture: The Gherkin and the Heron Tower

6 - City View

7 - Lord Mayor 2012 and the Lord Mayor's Coach

DAY7 KENSINGTON AND KNIGHTSBRIDGE

SECTION ONE

HYDE PARK WALK

1. Hyde Park Corner

This walk begins on an island at one of the busiest areas of London, Hyde Park Corner, with its imposing Wellington Arch, Apsley House (the home of the Duke of Wellington), and a host of war memorials.

Hyde Park Corner, officially entitled Duke of Wellington Place, is named after Arthur Wellesley, 1st Duke of Wellington, (1769–1852) renowned both for defeating Napoleon at the Battle of Waterloo in 1815, and for being Prime Minister of England in the late 1820s. A fine statue of him seated on his horse, Copenhagen is sited on the island facing Apsley House, the honey colored 18th century mansion to the north of the island on the edge of Hyde Park. Being the first house inside the Hyde Park Tollgate it was often referred to as Number 1 London. Today, it is home to the Wellington Museum and displays much Wellington memorabilia, Napoleonic artifacts in the basement as well as Wellington's collections of porcelain, fine paintings, furniture and medals. Undoubtedly the jewel of the museum is the magnificent 27 m (88.5 ft) Waterloo Chamber on the first floor where Wellington and his officers sat and dined each year on the anniversary of the Battle of Waterloo. The house, administered by English Heritage, opens Wednesday-Sunday and an entrance fee is charged. Refer to the website (*www.english-heritage.org.uk*) for up-to-date information and prices.

Dominating the centre of the island is Wellington Arch designed by Decimus Burton in the late 1820s as a triumphal arch to commemorate Wellington's victory over Napoleon. The Arch once housed a police station but is now used as an exhibition space open to the public and its balconies provide wonderful views looking out over the grounds and gardens of Buckingham Palace as well as the Royal Parks and Central London. From here you should be able to gain the best view of the gigantic bronze sculpture that surmounts the Arch, showing the Angel of Peace descending on the 4-horsed chariot of war.

If you time your visit carefully (around 10.30am Monday–Saturday; 9.30am Sunday) you may well see the procession of the Household Cavalry resplendent in their uniforms, mounted on impeccably groomed horses, riding through Wellington Arch en route to the Horse Guards Parade for the Changing the Guard ceremony. The soldiers leave their barracks in Hyde Park, ride to Hyde Park Corner, go through the Wellington Arch, along Constitution Hill into the Mall and then on to the Parade Ground. They return to the barracks about an hour later.

Whilst at this spot you might spend a few moments visiting the Commonwealth Memorials: The Australian War Memorial, Memorial to Commonwealth Troops and New Zealand War Memorial. Leave the traffic island on the west side close to the Royal Artillery Memorial, cross the roundabout and enter Hyde Park through the Portland stone screen adjacent to Apsley House.

2. Hyde Park *(standing on the corner of the park by the screen).*

Hyde Park, one of the four Royal Parks in Central London and the largest at 350 acres, was a Royal Hunting ground in the early 1500s, but is now a glorious oasis right in the centre of town and open to all. It extends to about 630 acres when combined with the neighbouring Kensington Gardens and boasts it own art galleries, lake, fountains, memorials and the famous 'Speakers' Corner. The park originally belonged to the monks of Westminster Abbey but when the land was seized by King Henry VIII after the Dissolution in the mid-16th century it became a Royal Hunting Park. It was first opened to the public in the reign of James I (1604–1625), developing into a fashionable resort during the reign of his grandson Charles II. Even so, deer were still hunted here until the mid 1700s. In Charles II's reign a circular drive and racecourse, 'The Ring' were established and much frequented by the in crowd in their stylish carriages.

In 1851 a major international trade fair, The Great Exhibition, was held on an area of 20 acres between Rotten Row and Knightsbridge (see map). An enormous palace of glass and iron was constructed for the event and ultimately became known as 'The Crystal Palace'. So tall was the building (it looked like a colossal greenhouse) that it enclosed huge trees and birds too. Within six months of opening almost a third of the population (some six million people) had visited and it is said that Queen Victoria herself attended the exhibition nearly every other day for three months! Later, the Crystal Palace was re-assembled in south London where it stood in a park until it burnt down in 1936. Sadly, it was never re-built. Profits made from the Exhibition were used in establishing the area between Hyde Park and South Kensington as a cultural and educational hub, a centre of museums and learning, nicknamed **'Albertopolis'**.

Hyde Park is always a popular venue for concerts: The Rolling Stones, Queen, Pink Floyd, Paul McCartney, Bruce Springsteen, Pavarotti and many other artists, both classical and pop have performed here. In 2012 during the Olympic Games special concerts were held in the Park at the opening and closing ceremonies and throughout the two week period giant screens broadcast events taking place elsewhere in the city. The park itself hosted the Triathlon and Marathon swimming events.

Such a large space naturally lends itself to festivals too: British Summer Time Hyde Park, a music and arts festival takes place here each summer, and in December the south east area of the park is taken over by 'Winter Wonderland', an extravaganza of fun fair rides, ice skating, Christmas market stalls, seasonal food and drink.

Throughout the year you will also see runners and walkers taking part in charity 5km and 10km events here.

The walk in the park covers its southern space but if you are keen to hear lively open air public speeches and debate then make your way up the path to the north-east corner to Speakers' Corner, close to Marble Arch. Although most activity takes place here on Sunday mornings this is the spot anyone can talk at any time, to anyone who will listen! The area was set aside for this purpose in the late 19th century and has accommodated orators and agitators like Karl

Marx, Vladimir Lenin, George Orwell as well as the Suffragettes in the run up to the First World War. Speakers are permitted to rant and rave about all manner of subjects including politics, religion, education and the economy so long as the content is considered lawful by the police.

3. Queen Elizabeth Gates and Achilles Statue

Located just inside the park, these brightly colored and decorated steel and bronze gates catch the eye with the vividly painted central red lion and white unicorn. Placed here to commemorate the 90th birthday of Her Majesty, Queen Elizabeth the Queen Mother they are one of many memorials within the Park. Almost adjacent is the bronze 6 m (20 ft) statue of Achilles, erected as a tribute by the Ladies of England Society, to the Duke of Wellington for his role in the victory over Napoleon at Waterloo. At the time of its construction in 1822 it was the most controversial of sculptures being the first nude public statue since Roman times! It caused such an outcry that it was deemed necessary to add a fig leaf to the statue after its installation, which remains to this day.

4. 7/7 Memorial

Located close to Park Lane, this memorial, in honor of those who died in the London bombings of 7 July 2005, commemorates each of the victims in 52 stainless steel pillars (stelae). The pillars are arranged in interlinking groups representing the four locations where people lost their lives and there is a plaque on the grass bank closest to the road listing their names.

5. Serpentine Bar and Kitchen

Ideal for a coffee stop or people watching location, the eatery offers snacks and hot dishes, patisserie and refreshments, and is right beside the lake with both inside and outside terrace dining areas.

6. Lakeside Walk

Stroll alongside the Serpentine Lake with the water on your right side. As you walk you can see the Boathouse on the north bank where pedalos and rowing boats are hired out and where you can take a trip between March and September in the Solarshuttle, a pleasure boat powered by the sun. Before long you will reach the Serpentine Lido, an area dedicated for public swimming during the summer. The Serpentine Swimming Club is the oldest in Britain and its members swim here every morning between 6 and 9.30am. Since 1864 members have taken part in a swimming race on Christmas Day (and since 1904, raced to win the Peter Pan Cup), in freezing cold waters usually below 4C! Swimmers have to train to become acclimatized in the months beforehand, and are cheered on by crowds of friends and spectators clothed in warm attire by the water's edge.

7. Rotten Row

South of the lake is a wide sandy tree-lined path often full of riders. This path, known as Rotten Row (derived from the French, 'Route du Roi' – the King's Road), was built in the 1690s for King William III as a link between his old home in Whitehall and his new palace at Kensington. At the time the park was a very dangerous place after dark with people being attacked and mugged by footpads and scoundrels. So the king ordered three hundred oil lamps to be hung from the trees along the path to light up the area and make it safe, and as such it became the first illuminated highway in the country. Today, local horse-riding stables bring their customers and members here and provide lessons for both children and adults.

8. Diana Memorial Fountain

Just beside the Lido and Café you come across an unusual water feature that was added to the park in 2004 to commemorate the life of Diana, Princess of Wales. Although entitled a 'fountain' it is more of an oval flowing waterway with small waterfalls and pools. You can sit on the edge of the memorial with your feet in the water or perhaps cross one of the three bridges to reach the core of the fountain. It is certainly relaxing to watch the water as it flows and cascades, supposedly a reflection of Diana's life.

9. Alternatives to the Walk in Bad Weather!
Serpentine Galleries:

These two art galleries focus on modern and contemporary art. The original 1970 gallery is housed in a classical Grade II listed former tea pavilion just to the west of West Carriage Road in Kensington Gardens, whilst the more recent 2013 addition, the Serpentine Sackler Gallery is found five minutes away to the north, just next to the Serpentine Bridge. Its home is in a restored 1805 former gunpowder store that has been extended to the design of the Pritzker Architecture Prize laureate Dame Zaha Hadid.

Both galleries open Tuesday–Sunday, 10am–6pm, and details of their current exhibitions are found on *www.serpentinegalleries.org*. The Serpentine Galleries emphasis is on emerging and establishing contemporary art and architecture and has exhibited works of many noted artists including Man Ray, Andy Warhol, Henry Moore, Bridget Riley, Wolfgang Tillmans and Damien Hirst. Since the millennium the Serpentine's annual architecture commission has showcased new temporary buildings by leading international architects. The architect has six months to complete a pavilion which is located on the lawn in front of the Serpentine Gallery for three months in the summer and is free to visitors to explore. In recent years Ai Weiwei, Jean Nouvel and Daniel Liebeskind have all presented their works here.

Exit Kensington Gardens via the Alexandra Gate. As you leave glance to your right to see the wonderfully flamboyant Albert Memorial, commemorating Queen Victoria's consort, Prince Albert (further details in Section 2).

THE SOUTH KENSINGTON MUSEUMS – EXHIBITION ROAD

As mentioned earlier, 'Albertopolis' is the name often applied to the area that stretches between Kensington Gardens, Hyde Park and South Kensington and is where three of London's finest museums, the Natural History, Science and Victoria & Albert are located. All were founded in the latter years of the 19th century and owe their origins to the Great Exhibition of 1851. The Exhibition which was remarkably successful had been the brainchild of Queen Victoria's husband, the Prince Consort, Prince Albert of Saxe-Coburg-Gotha, and it was the monies from the profits of the exhibition that were ploughed into this district to create resources for culture, learning and research. Imperial College, one of the world's top universities, renowned for its scientific and technical excellence and boasting 14 Nobel Laureates, is based here as well as the Royal College of Music, Royal College of Art, Royal Geographical Society, Royal Institution of Navigation, the Royal Albert Hall and the French Lycee.

The major draw of the area has to be its three outstanding museums and the Natural History and Science Museums are especially popular with children. As both are free to the public and open nearly every day of the year (except over the Christmas period), you might easily decide to 'dip into' both for a short time, though, be warned – there is just too much to see and do in one visit alone!

Note: This Section deals with the 2 museums mentioned above; Refer to Section Two for information about the Victoria & Albert Museum.

The Science Museum

This is an excellent museum to discover how and why things work, to learn about time, energy, space, the Information Age and the environment. Displaying everything from large transport and industrial machinery to lunar modules there really is something to keep everyone stimulated from toddler to senior citizen. With an IMAX and a 3D Motion Theater, flight simulators and the challenging interactive hands-on gallery Launchpad, there is much to fill the day.

Younger visitors are well catered for in the Garden and Pattern Pod areas, whilst the 'Who Am I?' gallery is irresistible for all with its exciting interactive exhibits. The 'Typhoon Force' simulator ride is a 'must-do' for anyone wanting to try their hand at flying a military jet and to experience at first-hand the adrenaline rush involved in conducting manoevres.

Apart from the permanent galleries the Museum regularly hosts temporary exhibitions: Past themes include 'Cosmonauts: Birth of the Space Age', 'the Large Hadron Collider' and 'Codebreaker: Alan Turing's Life and Legacy'. There is an extremely well-stocked shop on the ground floor selling a great variety of science based games, gadgets and experiments suitable for every age and budget. The museum also has a selection of cafes and a restaurant or if you prefer you can eat your own food in one of the designated picnic areas.

If you are in town on the last Wednesday of the month, the museum runs 'Science Museum Lates' – a themed night for adults offering live music, workshops and other entertainment.

The Natural History Museum

Right next door to the Science Museum on the corner of Exhibition Road and the Cromwell Road is the Natural History Museum (NHM), greatly loved by children and adults alike since opening in 1881. With a cathedral like interior and its stunning Romanesque exterior, Alfred Waterhouse's museum is one of London's most charismatic buildings. Stand outside its main entrance and look up towards the roof line and wonder at the fabulous statues and gargoyles carved in terracotta clay. Living creatures above the east wing, extinct animals, flora and fauna above the west wing. This gives a clue as to what lies within the building and is a fitting frontage to a museum dedicated to nature and the animal kingdom. Like the neighbouring Science Museum entrance is free and without a doubt, you will want to stay here for longer than you intend!

Famed in particular for its fantastic animated dinosaur displays, Creepy Crawlies and Mammals galleries, and for its gigantic life-size Blue Whale model, the museum has even more treasures to explore: discover a dodo skeleton, Igunadon (dinosaur) teeth, Apollo moon rock and even a Neanderthal skull – just a sample of the over 70 million specimens and artefacts held in the NHM's collections that date back over 4.5 billion years!

Today the museum displays these collection within 4 zones;

Blue Zone: Covers life on our planet with galleries dedicated to dinosaurs, sea and marine life, human biology and mammals

Green Zone: Relates to our environment, ecology and evolution.

Red Zone: (the former Geology Museum), contains the spectacular volcanoes and earthquakes gallery, and displays the earth's minerals, gems and crystals.

Orange Zone: is home to the new Darwin Centre, built to the west of the

main Waterhouse building, and houses over 20 million specimens. Here you can join NHM scientists to learn about moths, butterflies and birds or go on a Behind-the-Scenes Zoology Spirit Collection tour. There is a daily events calendar of tours, shows, talks and films and most are free.

You will find cafes and restaurants in each of the 4 zones and there are two shops within the NHM full of good quality goods and souvenirs. The Museum Shop, right by the front entrance stocks general gifts whilst the Cranbourne Boutique, beside the Deli café in the Red Zone, offers a great selection

of merchandise including small stones, jewellery and crystals. Regular exhibitions are held at the NHM. One of its most popular is the annual Wildlife Photographer of the Year Exhibition that draws huge throngs of visitors especially on weekends and during school holidays. Nonetheless, it is certainly worth the visit as you will see some wonderful and quite magnificent photographs of the natural world taken by ardent photographers determined to capture nature's wonders. Advance booking on-line is advisable if you want to miss the queues!

Another annual activity is the ice-rink which appears on the east lawn outside the museum from the end of October attracting people of every age and from all around the globe. Skating in this setting as dusk turns into night is a truly memorable experience and great fun too.

Harrods

No trip to London can be complete without a visit to this the most grandiose of stores. Harrods is without a doubt a real British institution. It covers in excess of 4.5 acres and with over a million square feet of selling space has become Europe's largest department store. Boasting 330 departments on seven floors, and selling everything from food to clothing, cosmetics, jewellery, designer goods and luxury gifts with a choice of nearly 30 eateries and bars, you may well find yourself spending an entire day here! The Food Halls are simply stunning and a pleasure to visit for their decoration (see the Royal Doulton tiles adorning the Meat Hall), visual presentation and breadth of produce from all corners of the world.

For gourmet-food lovers this is really an utter paradise and the there are plenty of treats to be purchased as gifts for friends, colleagues and family. Walk through the seven interconnecting food halls selling fish, meat, poultry and game, cheeses, tea, chocolates and confectionary, bakery products, biscuits, wines and jams and savour both the atmosphere and aromas. It is the place to find your ideal gift!

Harrod's motto is 'Omnia Omnibus Ubique' (All things, for all people, everywhere), and since it began trading in the 1830s the store has always prided itself on its superlative customer service and on supplying the highest quality produce and merchandise. Despite changes of ownership over the years the emphasis in providing the very best has remained unchanged. The store's owners constantly upgrade the building and its facilities keeping abreast of changing fashions and ensuring that they meet their customers' expectations. In the early 20th century the playwright Noel Coward was given an alligator bought from Harrods as a Christmas present, and in 1967, Ronald Reagan, former US president, received a gift of a baby elephant bought for him in the store from the son of King Zog of Albania.

Each year epic sales take place in Harrods in December and June/July. Offering fantastic discounts they attract huge numbers; in fact, as many as 300,000 customers may visit the store on the first day of the sale! For many years stars and celebrities 'opened' the sale, and it became an enormous international media event. Past 007 actors Roger Moore and Pierce Brosnan both carried out this role, as have singers Cher, Boyzone and Diana Ross and singer turned fashion designer, Victoria Beckham.

Harrods is open daily between 10am and 9pm Monday–Saturday, and 11.30am–6pm on Sunday and is easily accessible by tube (Knightsbridge Underground Station on the Piccadilly line), by bus (multiple routes), and has car parking facilities nearby.

The store is wonderfully illuminated at night and even more so at Christmas time when it is seasonally dressed up and you can see some fabulous window displays.

LONDON'S VILLAGES

HAMPSTEAD AND HIGHGATE

Now London suburbs, these villages were once a fair distance from central London and not considered part of the city. Both are situated on hills, command superb views and are easy to reach by underground, London Overground or bus.

In the 18th century Hampstead was popular as a spa town and it still retains some beautiful Georgian housing and shops. One of London's most fashionable and expensive suburbs today its appeal has much to do with its proximity to London as well as its green leafy surroundings.

Hampstead Heath is a large tract of ancient heath and parkland and a wonderful oasis so close to town. It's a joggers and dog walker's paradise, great for picnics and famed for its wonderful panoramic views of London. Intrepid bathers swim in its ponds which are also popular with anglers. To the north of the Heath is Kenwood House, an imposing 18th neoclassical villa boasting magnificent grounds with sloping lawns, lakes and flower gardens, Robert Adam interiors and with an excellent collection of paintings bequeathed to the country in 1927 by its owner, the 1st Earl of Iveagh. There is a good café in the adjoining Stable block and the house opens daily and is free to visit.

Highgate nearby is famous for its two Victorian cemeteries. Karl Marx is buried in the East side, whilst the West boasts the terrace catacombs and Egyptian Avenue and is where Douglas Adams, author of *The Hitch-hikers Guide to the Galaxy*, and Malcolm McClaren, rock-artist and clothes designer, are buried.

Richmond and Kew

Situated in south-west London these towns were both homes to royal riverside palaces in Tudor and Stuart times. **Richmond Palace** was a great favourite of Queen Elizabeth I where she died in 1603. Little remains of it today but the

magnificent royal hunting grounds have developed into Richmond Park, with red and fallow deer, grass and woodlands and ancient trees. The riverside town of Richmond is very pretty and boasts stunning Georgian architecture – doubtless the reason why so many celebrities from the world of music, acting, and political sphere live here. Residents include Jerry Hall, Richard E Grant, John Hannah, Peter Townshend, David Attenborough, Amanda Holden and Jane Horrocks.
Transport: Richmond (London Overground/District line tube)

Kew Palace can be visited in the grounds of the **Royal Botanical Gardens at Kew**, Opening in the summer months it is a delightful example of a royal country residence, surrounded by beautiful gardens and beside the river Thames. The Botanical Gardens, a UNESCO World Heritage Site, are simply stunning with the Victorian glass Palm and Temperate Houses as well as the 20th century Princess of Wales conservatory, filled with exotic plants and trees from all corners of the globe. There are play areas for children, exciting log and treetop trails as well as rhododendron, azalea and rose gardens and even a Chinese pagoda! You can see many very ancient and rare trees and there are also some very fine buildings notably the 18th century Orangery, now used as a restaurant, and the Marianne North Gallery. Here, the walls are full with the artist's numerous plant paintings from her travels in the 1800's in Australasia, Asia and the Americas, and the displays, as well as the building itself are quite unique.
Transport: Kew Gardens (London Overground/District line tube), Kew Bridge (South West trains)

Hoxton, Shoreditch, Brick Lane

This triangle of east London villages has changed out of all recognition in the past twenty or so years. Once one of London's poorest and neglected areas, close by London's docks and where the smelly industries were sited it is now the place to live, work and play. Warehouses have been turned into trendy apartments and work-spaces and the creative and technical industries have transferred here from the West End. Nearby, the junction of Old Street and the City Road is known as Silicon Roundabout and many start-ups are basing themselves in and around the area.

Busy both during the day and at night, the district is simply bursting with places to eat, bars, shops and galleries such as White Cube, the Geffrye Museum and Circus Space. Nearby Kingsland Road is the centre of Vietnamese cuisine, whilst Redchurch Street is awash with boutiques, cafes and shops.

This is certainly one of London's most fashionable spots right now: the place to see and be seen. There are themed bars and rooftop venues, markets galore (fashion, flower, flea, art and vintage clothing) as well as the super Bengali Indian restaurants in and around Brick Lane.

Transport: Liverpool Street (Circle, Metropolitan, Central, Hammersmith & City lines), Old Street (Northern line), Aldgate East (Hammersmith & City, District lines), Hoxton and Shoreditch High Street (London Overground).

Notting Hill and Chelsea

Notting Hill is probably best known for its annual summer carnival, a most vibrant and cosmopolitan 2 day event, when it seems that most of London is crammed into the tiny, narrow local streets eating, drinking, making music and enjoying life. You may also recognize the name from the 1999 Hugh Grant and Julia Roberts movie set in the area close to Portobello Road market. This is one of London's great markets and actually opens all week except Sunday; Saturday is its busiest day and is when all the antique stalls appear as well as specialist stalls and shops. The whole area is full of energy with crowds of people mingling and browsing among the rows of stalls and permanent street cafes, pubs and shops.

Transport: Ladbroke Grove (Hammersmith & City/Circle lines), Notting Hill Gate (Central, Circle & District lines).

The King's Road in Chelsea rather epitomizes the area: wealthy, chic, smart and forever filled with people shopping, eating and drinking! Originally a private road used by King Charles II to ride to his palace at Kew it is almost 2 miles in length stretching between Sloane Square and Fulham. In the 1950's and 1970's fashion designers Mary Quant and Vivienne Westwood had shops on the street and it was the haunt of many young teenagers eager to wear the latest fashions. The street is still home to independent designer shops although today you will also find high street chain shops as well. The Duke of York Square, home to the contemporary art Saatchi Gallery sits just west of Sloane Square, and offers a good selection of eateries and clothes shops. A short walk away is the **Royal Hospital Chelsea**, home of the Chelsea Pensioners, (men aged over 65 who have served as regular soldiers and are without any dependents), which is a delightful place to visit. Baroness Thatcher's rather simple grave is located in their graveyard and the Pensioners' infirmary, which she funded, is named after her. Facing the river Thames is Ranelagh Gardens, which becomes a hive of activity each May when it is the venue for the **Chelsea Flower Show.**

Transport: Sloane Square (Circle & District lines)

SECTION TWO

FROM KENSINGTON GARDENS TO THE VICTORIA AND ALBERT MUSEUM

A WALK THROUGH KENSINGTON GARDENS

Start at Lancaster Gate Underground Station. Cross over the Bayswater Road into Kensington Gardens

1. Lancaster Gate, Kensington Gardens. A brief history

One of London's eight Royal Parks, Kensington Gardens' landscape is mainly due to three royal queens, Mary II, Anne and Caroline, wife of King George II, all of whom left their own particular mark on it.

In 1689, Mary II, along with her Dutch husband, William III, created a palace garden in the Dutch style alongside their main London home, Nottingham House (now Kensington Palace). Their successor, Queen Anne, Mary's sister, enlarged the garden into a park and commissioned her gardeners, Henry Wise and George Loudon, to undertake alterations costing the vast sum of £26,000.

In the 18th century Queen Caroline gave Kensington Gardens a complete makeover and extended them by taking three hundred acres from Hyde Park! With her gardener, Charles Bridgeman, she introduced a ditch to separate the gardens from Hyde Park and this became known as a 'ha-ha' (as it was a surprise to come across it), and its use subsequently spread to estates throughout the land. At this time, the public had access to the park on Saturdays on the proviso that they wore respectable clothing! The Broad Walk, beside the palace understandably became the most chic place to be and be seen.

On ascending the throne in 1837 Queen Victoria moved her Court to Buckingham Palace resulting in few further improvements being made to the

Gardens during her reign apart from the creation of the Italian Gardens in the mid 19th century.

2. Italian Gardens

These splendid water gardens believed to be a present to Queen Victoria from Prince Albert are just one of the many attractions in this serene and elegant Royal Park. If the setting looks familiar do not be surprised as it is a favourite location for movie makers. Scenes from *Wimbledon* the tennis romantic comedy (2004) were filmed here as was the classic water fight scene between Bridget Jones's two rivals Daniel Cleaver and Mark Darcy (played by Hugh Grant and Colin Firth) in *Bridget Jones The Edge of Reason* (2004).

Close to the Italian Gardens you will find the initials of Queen Victoria and Prince Albert carved on the wall of the Pump House which once housed the steam engine used to operate the fountains.

Nearby you see the very first statue erected in the park in 1862. It remembers Edward Jenner, the 18th century doctor who pioneered the smallpox vaccine.

Walk to the end of the fountains and take the right hand path beside the Long Water.

3. Peter Pan Statue

The story of Peter Pan, the boy who can fly but never grows up is a much-loved favourite of children everywhere. It is said that its author, J M Barrie was inspired to write the tale after meeting and befriending the five young boys of the Llewelyn Davies family in Kensington Gardens in the 1890s.

Look closely at the charming bronze statue and you see Peter standing at its crest with fairies, mice, rabbits and squirrels, climbing up to him. Barrie, who wanted the statue to be a surprise on May Day for London's children, asked the sculptor, Sir George Frampton, to place it in the Gardens overnight. He achieved his aim and the statue still remains an utter delight to children (and grown-ups too!) over a century later.

4. Physical Energy

Almost in the very heart of the Royal Park, located towards the round pond is the grand and imposing equestrian statue, 'Physical Energy' by G F Watts, the celebrated Victorian sculptor and painter. It was installed here in 1907 as a memorial to Cecil Rhodes, the man who set up the De Beers mining company in the late 1800s and went on to establish Rhodesia, now Zimbabwe. A very wealthy man and a prominent figure during Queen Victoria's reign, Rhodes left his monies to Oxford University when he died and this became the basis for the Rhodes Scholarships, which allow for international postgraduate students to study at the university. Bill Clinton, (ex US president), Edwin Hubble (astronomer), Kris Kristofferson (musician/actor) and Terrence Malick (film director) have all been recipients of the award.

5. The Round Pond

This beautiful stretch of water was added to the Gardens when Queen Caroline began her renovation of Kensington Gardens into a park in 1728. Sited directly in front of Kensington Palace it is splendidly landscaped so that avenues of trees spread out in every direction and each provides a different view of the Palace. Although called the Round Pond, this is in fact a misnomer, as the pond is rectangular rather than circular in shape, albeit with rounded corners!

Always full of geese, ducks and swans the pond is also very popular with model yacht enthusiasts who come here Sunday mornings to race their craft. In fact, it has been the official home of the Model Yacht Sailing Association and London Model Yacht club for over 100 years.

6. The Broad Walk and Diana, Princess of Wales Memorial Playground

Before reaching Kensington Palace you cross a wide pathway, the Broad Walk, shared by pedestrians, cyclists, runners and joggers, thus making it a very busy thoroughfare. A slight diversion northwards (turn right along the Broad Walk) will lead you to the Diana, Princess of Wales Memorial Playground, established here in 2000. With its huge wooden pirate ship, tepees, beach cove and Indian camp, the playground has obvious associations with Peter Pan. It is an extremely popular play area and thousands of children come here, encouraged by the Peter Pan theme to rush about, play, imagine and simply enjoy the magic of Neverland.

Playing can be thirsty work – so it is fortunate that there is a café immediately beside the playground. Open all year it sells light meals and snacks and has a dedicated children's menu.

7. The Orangery

You will see this imposing building on your left just before you reach Kensington Palace. It was built for Queen Anne (1702-1714), as a very fancy palatial-style greenhouse, to house her citrus trees in the cold, frosty winter months. It later became a summer suppertime setting for entertaining guests, and its role as a dining venue continues to this day. Even if you don't eat there, do take a peek inside to look at the building's beautiful architecture boasting exceptionally high ceilings and windows. It opens daily between 10am and 6pm, offering breakfast and lunch as well as traditional afternoon tea, the only Royal Palace to do so in London.

8. Queen Victoria Statue

Situated between the Round Pond and Kensington Palace is a striking marble statue of Queen Victoria aged eighteen dressed in her coronation robes.

Designed by the Queen's artistic and talented daughter, Princess Louise, and placed here in 1893, the statue is a good starting point for your visit to Kensington Palace, childhood home of Queen Victoria.

9. Kensington Palace (www.hrp.org.uk)

Kensington Palace, a royal residence for over 300 years, is still home to members of our Royal Family, most notably, the Queen's grandson and his wife, the Duke and Duchess of Cambridge, and their children, Prince George and Princess Charlotte. Over the centuries since Nottingham House was transformed into a palace, it has housed both princesses and monarchs, but ceased to be a home for the sovereign in the 18th century. In recent years, both Princess Margaret (HM The Queen's younger sister), and Diana, Princess of Wales, lived at Kensington Palace and you will find portraits of each on displayed inside.

Joint monarchs, Mary II and William III were the first sovereigns to live here in the late 17th century, mainly on account of William's asthma. William was especially attracted by the fresh air of rural Kensington which he considered preferable to the dampness of the official London residence, Whitehall Palace, situated beside the River Thames.

A suite of rooms was built for each of the monarchs and these are open to visitors to the Palace today. The Queen's State Apartments date largely to the 1690s and consist of a group of rooms where Mary II and subsequent consorts lived. Although fairly plain today and no longer full of furnishings, it is easy to imagine what the rooms would have looked like and how cosy they must have been. In contrast, the King's State Apartments are far more decorated containing tapestries and works of art and sculptures. One painting by Vasari, much disliked by Queen Caroline, still hangs on the wall in the King's Drawing Room, despite her attempt to have it removed several centuries ago! Of all the rooms in the King's State Apartments the Cupola Room is outstanding for its ornamentation. Its octagonal shaped ceiling painted in blue and gold is quite magnificent and must certainly have been the most perfect setting for Queen Victoria's baptism ceremony. Both this room and the King's Staircase are the work of William Kent and were his first royal commissions. Kent's decoration of the King's Staircase is perhaps his most admired work in the Palace; the walls are painted with scenes of King George I's court and show all aspects of court life not purely the ceremonial and grand. In all over forty characters are depicted including courtiers and servants.

As Queen Victoria was born in the Palace on 24 May 1819 it is fitting that there is an exhibition devoted entirely to her, namely 'Victoria Revealed'. Here you will discover through quotes taken from the Queen's diary, details of her fascinating life, her unhappy childhood and gain an insight into her world. See displays including her wedding attire, and personal objects and find out about events during her exceptionally long reign (1837–1901). The exhibition also highlights the many roles she played as wife, mother, widow and monarch.

Before concluding your visit make sure to visit 'Fashion Rules', a temporary exhibition containing some of the iconic gowns worn by three members of the Royal Family: HM the Queen, Princess Margaret and Diana, Princess of Wales from the 1950s-1980s. The exhibition is a truly wonderful way to see the stunning clothing designed by some of the world's top fashion designers of the day and illustrates the changing fashions at the time when they were worn.

Royal Albert Hall and the Albert Memorial

Royal Albert Hall (www.royalalberthall.com)

The Royal Albert Hall (RAH) a mainstay of Albertopolis, is one of London's great multi-purpose venues. Not only a most distinguished building architecturally (built in the style of a Roman amphitheater), it also boasts a global reputation

for its range and exceptional quality of the programmes offered, especially the variety of concerts held within its auditorium. Its most famous concerts are the BBC Proms (Promenade Concerts), which run each year for an eight-week period between July and September. This is a daily music festival not to be missed; well-known classical pieces as well as newly commissioned music are played and it has always been the aim of its founders to reach as large an audience as possible, offering the greatest selection of high quality music.

The Proms season ends with the 'Last Night of the Proms', usually held on the second Saturday in September and sometimes a riotous affair with promenaders (those standing in the Arena), holding flags, banners and sporting rattles.

Since the RAH opened in 1871 it has always remained true to Prince Albert's original intention for a 'Central Hall' used to advance the Arts and Sciences. From the start it attracted famous musicians, composers, orchestras and singers, and artists like Shirley Bassey, Frank Sinatra, The Who, Sting, Elton John, The Beatles, Jay Z and One Direction have all had concerts here.

It is also a great venue for sporting events (tennis, boxing, Sumo-wrestling)

as well as rock and pop concerts, opera, circus and ballet. December sees a series of excellent Christmas carol concerts and recitals taking place in the auditorium and in January the circus troupe, Cirque du Soleil perform regularly to packed audiences. In addition, the Hall has hosted major public speeches of famous world leaders such as HM The Queen, Sir Winston Churchill, Nelson Mandela and former US President, Bill Clinton.

With the most fabulous interior design and decoration and outstanding terracotta façade (be sure to take note of the frieze), it is well worth taking one of the Royal Albert Hall guided tours. Here you can see not only the Front of House areas and auditorium, but also the Queen's private suite and the Royal Retiring Room. You will hear fascinating stories about people and events associated with the RAH and learn about the Victorian building and its architecture.

Albert Memorial (www.royalparks.org.uk)

Directly opposite the Royal Albert Hall sited just inside the boundary of Kensington Gardens is one of the Victorian era's most elaborate and some would say, gaudy memorials! A 'Gothic' shrine, designed by Sir George Gilbert Scott, it involved many of the leading sculptors and craftsmen of the day. The central focus of the memorial is the seated statue of Prince Albert holding a catalogue of the Great Exhibition in his hand and wearing the robes of the Knight of the Garter. Above him is a highly decorated canopy full of brightly colored mosaics and inscribed with the following words: 'Queen Victoria And Her People. To The Memory Of Albert Prince Consort. As A Tribute Of Their Gratitude. For A Life

Devoted To The Public Good'.

The memorial also contains an impressive frieze around its base showing noted artists, musicians, poets and writers.

With close to 200 sculpted figures the memorial is surrounded at the corners of the central area by carved figures representing Agriculture, Commerce, Engineering and Manufacture with further groups of figures and animals sited at the outer reaches and relating to Europe (with its bull), Asia (an elephant), Africa (a camel) and the Americas (a buffalo).

The shrine, honoring Prince Albert who died aged forty-two from typhoid, is a tribute to his dedication to and efforts in organizing the 1851 Great Exhibition. It was twenty years in the making and cost £120,000, an enormous sum of money at the time, and raised by means of public subscription.

Between March and December on the first Sunday of the month at 2pm and 3pm there are tours of the Memorial run by the highly knowledgeable and entertaining London Blue Badge Tourist Guides and these will allow you to go behind the protective railings and view the Memorial at close range.

The Victoria and Albert Museum – Exhibition Road

Here you will find the most wonderful and comprehensive collections of art, design and architecture and in a building that many suggest rivals its objects. Like the neighbouring Natural History and Science Museums, the Victoria and Albert (V&A) museum owes its existence to the Great Exhibition of 1851 and has occupied this site since the 1850s, becoming known as the V&A in 1899.

Laid out over 7 floors the museum's collections are vast and varied containing objects from across the world and from many different eras. There are galleries devoted to jewellery, silver and metalware, glass, ceramics, fashion and textiles, theater, carpets, sculpture, paintings, drawings and architecture and others of a geographical nature; displaying art of Asia, the Far East and the Islamic world.

One of the most fascinating spaces of the V&A is found within the two Cast Courts, double storeyed and purpose-built in the middle of the 19th century

to display casts (that is, copies) of some of the world's most famous buildings and sculptures. When the Courts were first built far less people travelled abroad than nowadays and so an exhibition of this type was a marvellous way to both complement the museum's own collections and to provide examples of the finest classical and Renaissance sculpture for the public and art students to learn from.

One of the most renowned of the casts is that of Michelangelo's 'David' (c.1856). Truly imposing at 6 m (20 ft) high its nudity was the cause of great consternation in the Victorian age. So much so, that for modesty's sake and to prevent offence to the queen it had a fig leaf added to it, whenever Queen Victoria or dignitaries visited the gallery. Although no longer in situ the fig leaf can still be viewed at the rear of the sculpture's plinth where it occupies its own special case!

Also in the these Courts you'll discover the most enormous cast of Rome's Trajan's Column, divided in two because of its height, the huge and striking doorway, 'Portico de la Gloria' from the Cathedral of Santiago de Compostela in Spain, as well as the pulpit from Pisa Cathedral and Medieval reliefs and Renaissance sculptures.

The display is very rare today as most similar museum collections abroad were dismantled in the early 20th century when attitudes changed towards their worth and/or importance. The V&A's casts are all the more valuable as a record of original carvings, many of which have weathered badly since they were first erected or have simply been lost during the intervening years.

Other museum treasures to look out for in your visit include:

- Tippoo's Tiger (South Asia Gallery), a scary wooden automated tiger savaging a British officer and from which, when a handle is turned, can be heard cries of anguish from the dying man.
- The Great Bed of Ware (British Galleries), a really gigantic 16th century oak bed measuring over 3 m (10 ft). The carved and commodious bed could accommodate at least four couples! Not only was it a tourist attraction in its own time but was also mentioned by Shakespeare in 'Twelfth Night'.
- The Ardabil Carpet (Room 42), the world's oldest, dated carpet. Emanating from Persia it is one of the largest most exquisite carpets in the world.
- The Becket Casket (Medieval & Renaissance galleries). Built to hold the relics

of St Thomas Becket the casket is a very beautiful object fashioned out of Limoges champlevé enamel. With a stunning blue and gold background the casket portrays the story of Becket's martyrdom.

- The Raphael Cartoons (Rooms 16, 26–27). Here you find 7 of the artist's full-scale designs for tapestries in the Vatican's Sistine Chapel, considered to be among the greatest gems of the High Renaissance period.
- Fashion Gallery (Room 40), where European fashion from 1750 to the present is displayed showing changing trends and clothing attire.
- Entrance Hall glass chandelier by American glass sculptor, Dale Chihuly. A most impressive monumental sculpture in blue, yellow and green it lights up the main hall especially on a dull day.

Naturally, in such a treasure trove the list of highlights is endless and much will depend on your own interests and tastes. It may be advisable to look at the

museum website (*www.vam.ac.uk*) in advance of your trip as this will give you some ideas for your visit as well as information about current exhibitions, talks and forthcoming events.

Alternatively, pick up a map and leaflet when you arrive for the daily events programme. Free introductory tours leave at 10.30am, 12.30, 1.30pm and 3.30pm daily and there are also regular tours of the Medieval and Renaissance, British, Theater & Performance galleries.

The museum caters well for its younger visitors running children's festivals, Family Art Fun Trails and activities as well as providing backpacks full of hands-on activities. Kids are seldom bored here and love the interactive displays, the opportunity to put on armour or dress up.

Before leaving the building a visit to the museum café on level 1 is highly recommended. Apart from providing refreshments the Victorian décor in the three interconnecting dining rooms is simply amazing. Each one is decorated in the most opulent manner and is the work of leading designers from the 19th century such as William Morris, Edward Burne-Jones and Philip Webb.

South Kensington underground station is less than five minutes walk away where trains (*Circle, District and Piccadilly lines*) will take you into Central London.

PICTURE CAPTIONS

1 - Wellington Arch, Hyde Park Corner

2 - The Household Cavalry, Hyde Park Corner

3 - Natural History Museum

4 - Roof Line Creature, Natural History Museum

5 - Harrods

6 - The Royal Albert Hall

7 - The Royal Albert Hall, Frieze

8 - Albert Memorial

9 - Victoria and Albert Museum: Medieval and Renaissance Gallery

10 - Victoria and Albert Museum: Original Refreshment Rooms

TRAVEL INTO AND AROUND LONDON

AIRPORT AND PORT TRANSFERS

It is easy to reach London from each of the 5 London airports (Heathrow, Gatwick, Luton, Stansted and City) as well as from the Channel and east coast ports. There are car-hire desks within the airports and signposts giving directions to buses, trains, taxis, the underground, and coach transport. Heathrow, Gatwick and Stansted each have dedicated express train services into central London, whilst Luton runs a train service to St Pancras where you can change onto the underground, and London City Airport connects to central London by the Docklands Light Railway (DLR).

If you're coming to London on the **Eurostar** service you will end your journey at **London St Pancras**, a major hub of the underground with six lines connecting to every part of town.

Passengers arriving at **Dover** can take three train services arriving at **Victoria**, **Charing Cross** or **London St Pancras**. The latter is the fastest service (some trains take a mere 65 minutes) but you pay slightly more for the convenience (about £30.00 single, £40.00 return), the other two take just under 2 hours and tickets cost less at about £22.00 single, or £35.00 return.

The train from **Harwich** connects with **Liverpool Street** with a journey time of about 82 minutes (including a change), and costs approximately £32.00 single, and £36 return (within a month). Liverpool Street is well-connected, serviced by four underground lines.

Airport Transfers

See below for information about transport services operating from each of London's airports, the journey length and indication of the costs of a single journey using the **£** symbol. Prices stated are current at time of going to press (2015).

Tickets: £ - £10 or less, ££ - £10.01-£20.00, £££ - £20.01+.

As always, it is best to check on-line for current information. If you are travelling by national rail you can buy tickets in advance from independent sellers like *www.thetrainline.com* often at a discounted price.

HEATHROW AIRPORT

Heathrow Express: Non-stop trains run to Paddington from Terminals 2 and 3.

London Underground: Piccadilly Line trains run from all terminals.

Heathrow Connect: Trains run to Paddington Station via local stations in west London.

National Express coach: Coaches run throughout the day, to Victoria coach station, central London.

Feltham rail link: The 285 bus links Heathrow with Feltham rail station, with trains into London Waterloo. Combined journey time is 100 minutes.

easyBus: This takes you to Waterloo via Shepherds Bush. Tickets can be booked in advance online, or subject to availability may be purchased from the driver (credit card payments only).

Taxis and Minicabs : London taxis are available outside each terminal. Minicabs are slightly cheaper.

Route	Approx frequency	Approx journey time	Approx cost
Heathrow Express	15 mins	21 mins	££
Heathrow Connect	30 mins	25 mins	££
Underground	5-10 mins	1 hour	£
Coach *	Every 5-30 mins	50-65 mins	£
easyBus	15 mins (peak)	65 mins	£
Taxi	On demand	30-60 mins	£££
Minicab	On demand	30-60 mins	£££

* National Express

GATWICK AIRPORT

The Gatwick Express: Non-stop train service to Victoria Station.

Southern trains: Train to Victoria Station via East Croydon and Clapham Junction.

Thameslink Services: Train to St Pancras International and Luton Airport, stopping at stations en route. Check timetable ** Note that no trains stop at London Bridge until 2018.

National Express: Direct coach service into London Victoria departing from both terminals at the lower level forecourt. Tickets available at National Express ticket desks in the terminals or in advance online.

easyBus: Departs from both North and South terminals into London Victoria coach station via Earl's Court/West Brompton. There is also a service from the South Terminal into Waterloo Station.

Taxis and Minicabs: Journey times and costs vary depending on your destination, There are taxi kiosks located in both terminals.

Route	Approx frequency	Approx journey time	Approx cost
Gatwick Express	15 mins	30 mins	££
Southern Trains	4 times an hour	30-35 mins	££
Thameslink	4 times an hour	30-45 mins	££
Coach *	Every 5-30 mins	90-120 mins	£
easyBus	15-20 mins	65 mins	£
Taxi	On demand	60+ mins	£££
Minicab	On demand	60+ mins	£££

* National Express

LUTON AIRPORT

Thameslink: Rail service linking Luton to central London, but you first need to take a shuttle bus from the airport to Luton Airport Parkway train station, about a 10 minute ride away. Follow airport signposts.

National Express/easyBus: Dedicated transfer into London over 60 times a day via Golders Green, St John's Wood, Baker Street into Victoria Coach Station.

Green Line Bus 757: Service into Victoria Coach Station

easyBus: Services run to **London Victoria Coach Station** and **Liverpool Street Station.** You will find EasyBus outside the main terminal building.

Taxi and Minicab: A taxi rank is located outside the Airport Terminal.

Route	Approx frequency	Approx journey time	Approx cost
Thameslink	6 trains an hour	45 mins	££
Green Line Bus	Every 30 mins day	60-90 mins	£
Coach *	60 services per day	50-65 mins	£
easyBus – Liverpool St	100 services per day	60 mins	£
Taxi	On demand	50-90 mins	£££
Minicab	On demand	50-90 mins	£££

* National Express/easyBus

STANSTED AIRPORT

Stansted Express: The train runs to Liverpool Street Station via Tottenham Hale.

easyBus: Operates service to **Baker Street** in the West End and another to the **City of London** (Old Street). Look out for the exit marked 'Buses'.

National Express: Services run 24 hours a day, stopping at 15 spots in London.

Terravision: Operates 2 buses, the A50 bus to London Victoria. The A51 to Liverpool Street Station via Bromley-by-Bow.

Taxi and Minicab Services: A taxi booking service is located in the international arrivals concourse operating 24/7. There is also a courtesy phone in the UK and Ireland baggage reclaim hall

Route	Approx frequency	Approx journey time	Approx cost
Stansted Express	15 mins	47 mins	£
Coach *	140 services per day	75-120 mins	££
easyBus to West End	15 mins	75 mins	£
easyBus to Old Street	15 minutes	60 mins	£
Terravision bus A50	Every 30 mins	75 mins	£
Terravision bus A51	Every 30 minutes	55 mins	£
Taxi	On demand	60+ mins	£££
Minicab	On demand	60+ mins	£££

* National Express

LONDON CITY AIRPORT

The Docklands Light Railway (DLR) departs every 8-15 minutes into central London from the airport. Using the Oyster Card it is an overground system and connects East London to the London Underground. Tickets are available at the DLR counter beside the Airport Terminal.

Black Taxi cabs and Minicabs

Licensed London Black taxis are available directly outside the Terminal building with fares into central London depending on your destination.

TRAVEL IN LONDON

To travel around London you will need to use one of the following: a **Visitor Oyster Card, Oyster Card,** a paper **Travelcard** or a **contactless payment card.** Both VisitLondon.com and Transport for London (TfL) explain the systems in detail on their websites, but a brief summary is given below:

A **Visitor Oyster Card** for use on the Underground (Tube), bus, DLR, London Overground, tram and many National Rail services in London, can be purchased in advance of your visit and delivered to your home address. The card costs £3.00 (non-refundable) plus postage and you select how much credit to add to it. This card will give you special offers and discounts during your stay for a number of London restaurants, attractions, shops, Thames Clippers river buses and on the cable car operated by Emirates Air Line. There is a daily price limit on the card so once you have reached it there is nothing more to pay.

An **Oyster Card** works in a similar way to the Visitor Oyster Card, but cost £5.00 (refundable), is only obtained in the UK and does not include any special promotions or offers. Cards are available from Visitor Information Centres (at Heathrow and Gatwick Airports, Paddington, King's Cross, Euston & Victoria mainline stations, and Liverpool Street & Piccadilly Circus tube stations), and at Oyster Ticket Stops in many newsagents and shops.

Contactless Payment Cards are debit, credit or pre-paid cards and may be used as payment for a ticket up to a £20.00 limit. There is no need to use a PIN or a signature. If your contactless card has been issued outside the UK you should first check if your bank charges transaction fees for usage on the London transport system.

Paper Travelcards, like Oyster Cards, can be used on the Underground (Tube), bus, DLR, London Overground, tram and many National Rail services in London. They will cover certain zones (London is divided into Zones 1-9) and last for 1 day only. As with a Visitor Oyster Card you will obtain discounts on various river boat services and also on the Emirates Air Line cable car.

A 7 day Travelcard is also available but can only be loaded on to an Oyster Card.

When using Oyster Cards and Contactless Payment Cards you **must** touch the yellow card reader at the gates at the start and end of your journey or you could get charged a **penalty fare.**

On **buses and trams** you only need to touch the yellow card reader at the **start** of your journey. **Note:** Only Oyster Cards or Contactless Payment Cards can be used on buses. No cash is accepted.

Credit can be added to your Oyster or Visitor Oyster Card at the touchscreen ticket machines in Tube, London Overground, DLR and some National Rail Stations, at Oyster Ticket Stops, from Visitor and Travel Information Centres and Emirates Air Line Terminals.

Transport for London (TfL) Buses

These are mainly the classic double-decker red buses that London is renowned for, and are good to use around the centre of town. Information about timetables and routes is available on the TfL website, but it may be useful to know that Buses No 11 & 15 run past most of the tourist hotspots:

- 11: From Liverpool Street via the City to Victoria, Sloane Square, the Kings Road to Fulham Broadway
- 15: From Trafalgar Square to Blackwall via Tower Hill and Aldgate

Private Tourist Buses

There are several hop-on/hop-off 24 hour services offered with live commentary in English as well as recorded information in a number of languages. Ranging in price between £25 and £30 this can be a good way to see many of the sights if you are only in London for a short time.

Black Taxi Cabs and Minicab services

You will see black cabs everywhere and fares are determined by the length of the journey and time of day. Other cab services include Uber, Addison Lee as well as local minicab hire, details of which can be found online.

Santander Cycles

This is certainly a cheap way to get round London. You can hire a Santander Cycle for as little as £, ideal for short trips. You just need to take a credit or debit card to the docking terminal and follow the instructions on the screen. All journeys after the first one are free within 24 hours if they last less than 30 minutes each. Refer to the TfL website *www.tfl.gov.uk* for more information about the self-service bicycle hire scheme.

Travel websites:

easyBus	www.easybus.com
Gatwick Express	www.gatwickexpress.com
Green Line Bus	www.greenline.co.uk
Heathrow Express	www.heathrowexpress.com
Heathrow Connect	www.heathrowconnect.com
National Express	www.nationalexpress.com
National Rail	www.nationalrail.co.uk
Southern Trains	www.southernrailway.com
Stansted Express	www.stanstedexpress.com
Terravision	www.terravision.eu
Thameslink	www.thameslinkrailway.com

WEB ADDRESSES

Day 1:

www.london.gov.uk	Parliament Square
www.westminster-abbey.org	Westminster Abbey
www.parliament.uk	Houses of Parliament, Big Ben, Elizabeth Tower, Portcullis House
www.hrp.org.uk	Banqueting House
www.gov.uk	Downing Street
www.householdcavalrymuseum.co.uk	Household Cavalry Museum
www.changing-guard.com	Horseguards
www.royalparks.org.uk	St James's Park, Hyde Park, Regent's Park
www.royal.gov.uk	St James's Palace, Buckingham Palace
www.royalcollection.org.uk	Royal Mews, Queen's Gallery

Day 2:

www.coventgarden.uk.com	Covent Garden
www.actorschurch.org	St Paul's church, Covent Garden
www.ltmuseum.co.uk	London Transport Museum
www.roh.org.uk	Royal Opera House
www.sevendials.co.uk	Seven Dials
www.sohotheater.com	Soho Theater
www.tkts.co.uk	Half-price Theater Ticket booth
www.visitlondon.com	Piccadilly Circus, Leicester Square
www.chinatownlondon.org	ChinaTown

www.london.gov.uk	Trafalgar Square
www.britishmuseum.org	British Museum
www.templechurch.com	Temple Church
www.innertemple.org.uk	Inner Temple
www.middletemple.org.uk	Middle Temple
www.nicholsonspubs.co.uk	The Blackfriar Pub

Day 3:

www.hrp.org.uk	The Tower of London
www.skdocks.co.uk	St Katharine Dock
www.towerbridge.org.uk	Tower Bridge
www.rmg.co.uk	Royal Maritime Greenwich
www.greenwichwhs.org.uk	Maritime Greenwich, World Heritage Site
www.the-shard.com	The Shard
www.theviewfromtheshard.com	The View From The Shard
www.londoneye.com	Coca-Cola London Eye

Day 4:

www.somersethouse.org.uk	Somerset House
www.courtauld.ac.uk/gallery	Courtauld Gallery
www.tate.org.uk	Tate Galleries: Tate Modern, Tate Britain
www.shakespearesglobe.com	Shakespeare's Globe Theater
www.southbankcentre.co.uk	Southbank Centre
www.bfi.org.uk	British Film Institute
www.nationaltheater.org.uk	National Theater

www.oxotower.co.uk	Oxo Tower
www.banksidegallery.com	Bankside Gallery
www.goldenhinde.com	Golden Hinde II
www.clink.co.uk	Clink Prison Museum
www.cathedral.southwark.anglican.org	Southwark Cathedral
www.boroughmarket.org.uk	Borough Market
www.george-southwark.co.uk	The George Inn

Day 5:

www.oxfordstreet.co.uk	Oxford Street
www.selfridges.com	Selfridges
www.regentstreetonline.com	Regent Street
www.liberty.co.uk	Liberty
www.carnaby.co.uk	Carnaby Street
www.hamleys.com	Hamleys
www.nationalgallery.org.uk	National Gallery
www.npg.org.uk	National Portrait Gallery
www.lockhatters.co.uk	Lock & Co
www.bbr.com	Berry Bros and Rudd
www.fortnumandmason.com	Fortnum & Mason
www.florislondon.com	Floris
www.paxtonandwhitfield.co.uk	Paxton and Whitfield
www.royalacademy.org.uk	Royal Academy
www.bondstreet.co.uk	Bond Street
www.roccofortehotels.com	Brown's Hotel

Day 6:

www.stpauls.co.uk	St Paul's Cathedral
www.cityoflondon.gov.uk	The Guildhall, Guildhall Art Gallery
www.onenewchange.com	One New Change
www.bankofengland.co.uk	Bank of England
www.cityoflondon.gov.uk	Mansion House, Leadenhall Market
www.theroyalexchange.co.uk	Royal Exchange
www.stlawrencejewry.org.uk	St Lawrence Jewry Church
www.cityoflondon.gov.uk	St Mary Aldermanbury Church & Gardens
www.smithfieldmarket.com	Smithfield Market
www.greatstbarts.com	St Bartholomew the Great Church
www.museumoflondon.org.uk	Museum of London

Day 7:

www.english-heritage.org.uk	Wellington Arch, Apsley House
www.royalparks.org.uk	Hyde Park (Royal Parks)
www.sciencemuseum.org.uk	Science Museum
www.nhm.ac.uk	Natural History Museum
www.harrods.com	Harrods
www.royalparks.org.uk	Kensington Gardens
www.hrp.org.uk	Kensington Palace
www.royalalberthall.com	Royal Albert Hall
www.royalparks.org.uk	Albert Memorial
www.vam.ac.uk	Victoria & Albert Museum

Useful websites:

www.visitlondon.com

www.timeout.com

www.thelondonist.com

www.royal.gov.uk

www.culture24.org.uk

GLOSSARY

Historical Periods

Roman	AD43-410
Tudor	1485-1603
Stuart	1603-1714
Georgian	1714-1837
Victorian	1837-1901
Edwardian	1901-1910

Art and Architectural terms:

Art-deco: An architectural and decorative style of the 1920s and 1930s using vibrant colors and patterns.

Art Nouveau: A popular style between 1890-1910 often characterised by its curves and swirling decoration.

Baroque: A flamboyant and monumental architectural style in fashion around 1600 to 1750.

Brutalist: An architectural style of the mid-late 20th century using rough concrete and large massive blocks.

Edwardian: Styles mainly in use during the reign of King Edward VII (1901-1910), such as Gothic Revival, Neo-Georgian, Baroque Revival, Arts and Crafts Movement.

Georgian: The style of art and architecture between 1714 and 1830 during the reigns of George I, II III and IV when classical proportions were introduced into all types of buildings.

Gothic: Referring to the style of the Middle Ages and renowned for its pointed arch, rib-vaulting and large windows.

Palladian: Properly formulated elegant and classical architecture introduced into England from the early 17th century.

INDEX

IMAGE INDEX

Unless indicated below all photographs in this book are © A McMurdo

Builders

Page 132 : Borough Market © VisitEngland/Diana Jarvis / Visit England

Page 145 : Walkie Talkie Sky Garden © Rhubarb

Page 186 : St Michael's Alley, Jamaica Wine House © VisitEngland/City of London/Clive Totman / City of London/Clive Totman

Page 188 : City Architecture: The Gherkin and the Heron Tower © VisitEngland/ City of London/Clive Totman / City of London/Clive Totman

Page 188 : City View © Rhubarb

Page 196 : Lord Mayor 2012 and the Lord Mayor's Coach © Jamie Smith

Page 225 : Victoria & Albert Museum: Medieval & Renaissance Gallery © Victoria and Albert Museum, London

Page 227 : Victoria & Albert Museum: Original Refreshment Rooms © Victoria and Albert Museum, London

Back Cover : The State Opening of Parliament Procession 2013 © VisitEngland/ Diana Jarvis /

Back Cover : Chimneys, Hampton Court Palace © Historic Royal Palaces

ACKNOWLEDGMENTS

I would like to thank all the staff at New Holland Publishers who have been involved in the production of this book, especially Alan Whiticker and Jessica McNamara.

I am also indebted to Michelle Wood from VisitEngland, Andrew Buckingham and Mick Bagnall from the City of London Corporation for their help and advice. In addition I would like to thank staff at VisitGreenwich, VisitBrighton, Middle Temple, Southwark Cathedral, Temple Church, the Victoria & Albert Museum, the National Theatre, Coin Street Community Builders, St Katharine Dock, Historic Royal Palaces, the Royal Opera House, Blue Rubicon, The Canal & River Trust, The George Inn and Somerset House for their help in sourcing images.

My thanks too to Bob Brown, Yeoman Warder, at the Tower of London and Chelsea Pensioners, Simon de Buisseret and Joe Hutt for allowing me to photograph them and include their images in the book.

Sadly, there is not enough space to highlight everyone who has helped on this project but I would like to say a particular thank you to Peter Darby, Joanna McMurdo, Ben McMurdo and Janet Shropshall, who had the arduous task of proof-reading and providing valuable feedback.

Finally, my greatest thanks go to my husband, Mac. He not only pounded the streets alongside me, taking many photos on the way, but has always been unfailingly enthusiastic and an excellent sounding board whilst I wrote the book.

First published in 2016 by New Holland Publishers Pty Ltd
London • Sydney • Auckland

The Chandlery Unit 704 50 Westminster Bridge Road London SE1 7QY United Kingdom
1/66 Gibbes Street Chatswood NSW 2067 Australia
5/39 Woodside Ave Northcote, Auckland 0627 New Zealand

www.newhollandpublishers.com

A record of this book is held at the British Library and the National Library of Australia.

ISBN 9781742577951

Managing Director: Fiona Schultz
Publisher:Alan Whiticker
Project Editor: Anna Brett, Jessica McNamara
Designer: Andrew Quinlan
Production Director: James Mills-Hicks
Printer: Toppan Leefung Printing Ltd

10 9 8 7 6 5 4 3 2 1

Keep up with New Holland Publishers on Facebook
www.facebook.com/NewHollandPublishers